ASSEMBLED IN LIGHT

"Architecture is a learned game, correct and magnificent, of forms assembled in the light." —Le Corbusier

ASSEMBLED IN LIGHT

The Houses of Barnes Coy Architects

Alastair Gordon
Barbara de Vries

foreword by Pilar Viladas
principal photography by Michael Mundy

Rizzoli New York
New York Paris London Milan

for

Robert M. Barnes

(1950–2018)

CONTENTS

PREFACE

Christopher Coy

The true preface is to say that Rob Barnes is no longer with us. He passed away unexpectedly during the development of this book, and now the book itself must stand as a tribute to Rob's exceptional career as an architect, as well as being a celebration of our twenty-five-year partnership, and a critical look at the firm's residential work over the past decade.

The essence of the Barnes Coy method evolved from an unusually close collaboration between the two of us. Rob and I would work at a simple trestle table that occupied the space between our desks, seated across from each other, sketching on the same length of tracing paper. We were like counterweights, balancing as well as tempering our concepts, while reinforcing each other's thought processes.

We both believed that residential architecture is the true front line of modernism, and that a house can be much more than the sum of its parts. People live in these houses. They relax, work, and raise families in these houses. Each and every family is like a little country unto itself, with its own territories, secrets, and rituals. We work to understand these personal rituals and permit them to inform our designs. Architecture is an integrative art form: space acquires meaning when it is layered with definition.

Rob and I attended a boarding school that was run by English Benedictine monks, and we became acquainted with monastic life. As much as we rebelled against it, we recognized a certain nobility to giving up the comforts of life in order to pursue a spiritual truth. As Moshe Safdie said, "Seek beauty and you will find only vanity. Seek truth and you will find beauty." If your frame of reference is a commitment to truth—truth in form, structure, and light—then your architectural response is always going to come out of that same place.

Despite his sharp, often irreverent sense of humor, Rob was a spiritual seeker in his own way. This came through in his architectural practice and the close relationships he developed with clients, how he listened to their needs and worked to fulfill their dreams of domestic tranquility. In this way, he also served as something of a priest or spatial guru, offering revelatory experiences of space and light, as well as a chance for self-discovery.

Despite the tragic loss of my business partner and lifelong friend, Barnes Coy Architects continues to be committed to innovation and the creation of harmonious domestic spaces that celebrate light and the elegance of a modernist sensibility. First and foremost, we believe that architecture must be beautiful.

Alastair Gordon is uniquely qualified to write this book. He is both an old friend and a serious and celebrated critic of architecture and observer of art and culture, who has known Rob and me for as long as we knew each other. In fact, the three of us met on the same day on the beach when we were ten years old. Alastair brings a deep understanding of how the Barnes Coy working relationship was informed by our friendship outside the studio. Pilar Viladas's foreword illuminates the basic themes behind our architecture, specifically those inherent in residential architecture.

This book is dedicated to the memory of Robert Barnes, the best man at my wedding, godfather to my daughter, Camille, and my best friend and working partner. May he rest in peace.

FOREWORD

Pilar Viladas

For Barnes Coy Architects, designing houses is almost "a spiritual calling," says Christopher Coy, one of the firm's founding partners. In the years after Coy and Robert Barnes established the firm in 1993, the two architects came to realize that in the professional world of architecture, houses were perceived as "lesser" compared to large projects like office buildings or museums. Barnes and Coy believed that designing a house was on the very front lines of architecture. They had been good friends since the age of ten and went to the same boarding school. Until Barnes's untimely death in 2018, they would talk about architecture every workday over lunch, and both felt that the house was a particularly intimate building type. "It's where you have your most personal moments," Coy says. "It contains elements of every building type." But the combined weight of all this symbolism makes the house typology more fraught, according to Coy, especially in the expansive, and expensive, houses that the firm became known for, where the clients' expectations are particularly high. But given the number of repeat clients—the firm has done six projects for one of them—Barnes Coy has clearly demonstrated a mastery at integrating the emotional and the architectural.

One of the firm's core beliefs is that a design always starts with the site. In addition to the numerous oceanfront houses Barnes Coy has designed, there are also houses in the mountains of Colorado, in the California desert, and on a cliff in Costa Rica, to name a few of the firm's diverse settings. While each site presents its own constraints—oceanfront houses, for instance, are designed and built to strict local and federal codes to protect buildings from hurricane damage and dunes from erosion, while California's seismic codes demand another kind of structural response—Coy says, "We choose to look at these constraints as design opportunities." One Long Island beach house, for example, was required to be set well back from the dunes and ocean and this inspired the architects to design angled walls and windows for parts of the house that don't have a direct ocean view, offering glimpses of the water that were no less poetic for not being panoramic.

But these exigencies are secondary to creating a sense of place that comes from the site itself. In the California house, for example, two opposed, starkly geometric forms are as rugged as the mountains in the distance. For the house in Costa Rica, the architects designed a narrow, suspended walkway that extends beyond the deck to hover over a view of the ocean below. Barnes Coy's designs may be respectful of their settings, but they're never recessive; they defer to the site but are emphatic frames for their surroundings.

From the beginning of their partnership, Barnes and Coy were committed to working in a modernist architectural vocabulary, believing, as Coy says, "that modernism is an intervention for which no excuses can be made." And in places like the Hamptons, where sprawling interpretations of historic Shingle Style and Colonial houses outnumber contemporary versions by a good margin, the firm's houses are unapologetically rooted in the present. Strong rectilinear and curvilinear forms define the architecture, and the materials are a blend of rugged and luxurious. An interior wall of board-formed concrete, for instance, reflects not only the toughness of the material, but also the sensuous grain of the wooden boards used to form it. And a meticulous approach to detail is apparent in the elegantly recessed railing of a stairway in a house in Water Mill, New York, or the full-height oak doors in another Long Island house that are designed without doorframes, to be flush with the wall. This focus on the craft of building speaks to what Coy describes as the firm's second core belief: "Architecture should be the art of built work, not drawings or models."

"Materials," Coy says, "are a constant learning curve for us." He believes that contemporary architecture, just like more traditional buildings, should still look good in fifty or a hundred years, and bemoans materials that don't age well, something he considers to be the "scourge" of twentieth-century modernism. Having used rough fieldstone in some of their early projects, the architects eventually began to use cut stone as cladding. Quarried in the United States, France, and India, it produces a tighter and cleaner line, and can, as Coy says, "follow the forms as they weave inside and outside the glass line, which is one of our preferred methods of expressing interior/exterior fluidity." Lately, the architects have used more wood, metal panels, and porcelain slabs on exteriors, as well as stucco, for which they employ a complex construction system and a hand-sanded topcoat that gives the material a stonelike finish. However, not all the materials Barnes Coy uses are state-of-the-art. For a house on a barrier island in Georgia, the architects used columns made of forty-foot cypress tree trunks that were found submerged in a swamp.

In contrast to the cutting-edge building methods they employ, Barnes Coy's office is structured in a comparatively old-fashioned way. The deliberately small staff of fourteen is spread between two offices, in Bridgehampton and Manhattan, and is intentionally an international mix. Coy works closely with the four senior architects who have worked there an average of fourteen years, a low rate of turnover. "I want to tap their talents," says Coy, who believes in paying architects well, and in establishing a workplace that more closely resembles a studio. "Rob and I never wanted to become managers; we wanted to be architects," he says.

This structure grew logically out of Barnes and Coy's fairly atypical partnership. Between their private offices was a central trestle table at which they shared ideas and worked out design schemes, while a window wall offered a view of the woods beyond. For the two men, ego "was not an issue," Coy says, adding that their shared commitment to modernism and to creating family spaces made it easy to work together. Occasionally, when a project proved especially difficult to design, they would embark on a ritual they called "the dark night of the soul," in which they would go to the office on Saturday morning, work until late at night, breaking only for take-out food, and would, if necessary, return on Sunday morning for more of the same. Coy attributes this work ethic to the "self-denying, ascetic approach" of the Benedictine monks who were their teachers at boarding school.

This working relationship defied their clients' assumptions about how architects functioned, and they were often asked which one of them was "the practical guy," as opposed to the more idealistic, design-focused partner, but they shared equal responsibilities in every aspect of the design process. "We wanted clients to feel the strength of our partnership," Coy explains. "If one of us was not there, you could talk to the other one about anything."

Though they always kept a close eye on budgets and construction schedules, they never wanted to waste their design time tracking expenses and profitability. This design-focused philosophy produced house after house that, for all their architectural bravura, consistently convey the sense of shelter and domesticity that the architects always held—and which Coy continues to hold—so dear.

POINTS OF INFLECTION

Alastair Gordon

Le Corbusier spoke of "forms being assembled in light," and light creating the expression of a structure, something that Robert Barnes and Christopher Coy—cofounders of Barnes Coy Architects—have explored throughout their twenty-five-year partnership. They both grew up on eastern Long Island and came to understand the special qualities of light out east, that same watery radiance that lured artists like Jackson Pollock and Willem de Kooning to the Hamptons after World War II.

Although there may not be a single, recognizable Barnes Coy style, there are distinctive themes and architectural tropes that appear in their work. Early on in their partnership, they learned that forms were defined in light, and that light can become an active participant in the design process. "One thing light does is carve the forms of our architecture," said Coy. "Light is everything," said Barnes.

They work with minimal forms, transparency, and rugged textures to capture, express, and shape the natural light, almost as if it were a malleable substance. Flying beams, cantilevered overhangs, and outrigger-type elements are used to throw webs of shadow across exterior surfaces. Spatial clusters unfold at opposite ends. In plan, one senses a restless movement of angled planes, staggered rooflines, and shifting volumes. Orthogonal meets oblique. Perimeter barriers are stepped back and penetrated by walkways, terraces, and pergolas. Raised decks and infinity pools further delineate the edgeless edge.

The idea was to create a sense of suspension, the momentary illusion of levitation, a restless, drifting sensation, a kind of dematerialization in which corners and tapered edges appear to melt away. Rooflines are eggshell thin and cantilevered outward, as if hovering in midair. Structural membranes and floor plates are fully revealed. Windows wrap all the way around the perimeter. Curtain walls of sheer glass meet flush at specially engineered corners. The house turns itself inside out. Forms punch through other forms. The skeletal framework becomes a sculptural armature, revealed and exploited. Centrifugal forces are offset by centripetal forces, concave forms by convex. Ethereal moments of flotation are placed in contrast with a sometimes-queasy twisting of axes, and the use of contrasting forms in the tradition of late Cubism and the Purism of Léger, Ozenfant, and Le Corbusier, in which curvilinear plays against rectilinear.

"We learned that everyone enjoys the blurring of inside and outside, and we try to help our clients discover that for themselves,"

opposite page: Oceanfront House, Southampton, New York.

said Coy. "Everyone loves a loggia. Everyone loves a pergola. Everyone loves to sit in a sheltered space that's open to the outside. It's basic human nature."

What comes across is a certain livability, a smoothness and relaxed sense of comfort. These are not soulless Hamptons trophy houses competing for attention against other mega-mansions along the beach. They are modern but never cold or clinical. They breathe, expand, and contract as places of family gathering and reflection. They are warm, human, and sustainable.

The architects pride themselves on becoming lifelong friends with many of their clients. "There's always a give-and-take," said Coy. "We try to listen to our clients' ideas. Our favorite thing is when we get a thank-you note from one of them saying how they never understood what we were doing until they moved in and experienced the spaces for themselves. They didn't know the view would look like this or that the light would filter in that way. Our most satisfying comment is always: 'We're so happy to be here.' In the end that's what we're trying to do."

There's often some kind of a bridge, a modern-day moat that the architects use to ritualize the approach to the entry. Such bridge-like elements are used to negotiate a transition in grade, create a heightened sense of entry, or simply to emphasize direction. "Bridges are the most beautiful structures ever built, whether it's a rope bridge in Peru or the George Washington Bridge," said Coy. "It's the beauty of a suspended pathway rising above some natural obstacle: a ravine, gully, river, whatever."

Notable examples were used with several Hamptons houses, but the most conspicuous is at "Cielo Mar" in Costa Rica, where the transitional gesture becomes an actual suspension bridge that projects out toward the Pacific Ocean. A more restrained version was employed at the Meadow House in Sagaponack, where a raised walkway of teak traverses the central courtyard and creates the feeling of ceremonial arrival.

The architects have also worked with different kinds of grounding devices around which the rest of the house evolves both structurally and symbolically. Interior spaces are often punctuated by distinctive sculptural elements that might take the form of a staircase or a fireplace-chimney mass. At one beachfront house, the staircase takes on a central role. Railings of curved steel and steps of white oak rise up through an elliptical void and create a spatial armature around which the rest of the house unfolds.

"It's exciting to see such a highly articulated object rising in the middle of an open, transparent space," said Coy, whose favorite method of fabricating a staircase is to take a long sheet of steel and have it folded into zigzagging steps. "It's a bold but simple way to animate an interior space."

The fireplace can become an extended wall that divides interior space while making a dominant presence that helps ground the often floating and aerial quality of the architecture. Thoreau spent three chapters in Walden philosophizing about the sacred hearth because he had to keep from freezing and he needed to cook, and the hearth was one of the themes that ran through all of Frank Lloyd Wright's work.

"What's the first thing you do in a cave or a primitive hut?" asked Coy. "You create a place to get warm and cook your food." When Coy was living in a cave on the Canary Islands in the 1970s, the first thing he did was build a primitive fireplace out of rocks.

Rob Barnes was born at the Nassau Hospital in Mineola, Long Island, on July 15, 1950. His mother, Betty, was a descendent of Benjamin Rush, a signer of the Declaration of Independence. His father, Robert, was a successful builder and real estate developer. Christopher Coy was born six months later, on December 19, at the Hackensack Hospital, and he grew up in Ramsey, New Jersey. His father, James, was a commercial banker who worked for James Talcott Inc. His mother, Evelyn, was the daughter of Albert Poppiti, a municipal sculptor who created many well-known monuments in New York City and Washington, DC.

Barnes and Coy first met on the beach in East Hampton when they were ten years old. They attended the Junior Yacht program, a summer day camp at Devon Yacht Club, and would go swimming off the end of a long dock and sail across Gardiners Bay on Sunfish and WoodPussy catboats.

The art of the house was deeply embedded in Rob Barnes's DNA. He grew up in the building business and was fascinated by all aspects of residential architecture. His great-grandfather (Robert) started the Barnes Building Company in the late nineteenth century. Among other civic projects, he built the New York State Capitol in Albany, a massive Romanesque Revival building designed by Henry Hobson Richardson that featured flamboyant towers, ornate dormers, and rustic limestone walls. Rob's father (also named Robert), took over the business and built more than five hundred houses, from Garden City—where the family had a year-round home—out to the eastern tip of Long Island.

Robert Barnes Sr. had a basic set of assumptions about what people needed in their family homes: so many square feet of living space for such and such an amount of money, all of it based on a predictable formula. He knew what his clients wanted, and most were fairly conventional houses without surprises, basic "builder's specials," that were easy to build, easy to sell, and designed in a variety of neo-traditional styles, from cookie-cutter Cape to Colonial and neo-Tudor, filling in the lots of so many suburban subdivisions across Nassau and Suffolk counties. (In 1952, he built a low-lying ranch house with a two-car garage for his mother-in-law on Hunting Lane, East Hampton.)

Rob would grow up to become an outspoken critic of the generic houses his father built, but occasionally Robert Senior worked with an architect who challenged all of his assumptions about what an American house could be. In 1967, when Rob was seventeen years old, his father began work on an unusual commission for Bertram and Phyllis Geller, at 339 Ocean Avenue, in Lawrence, Long Island. The 4,500-square-foot house featured a wide-span concrete vault roof, soaring interior spaces and flagstone floors. (Concrete work was done by Azzarone Construction.) The architects were Marcel Breuer, Bauhaus legend and former associate of Walter Gropius, in collaboration with Herbert Beckhard. (It was the second house that Breuer designed for the Gellers. The first, also located in Lawrence, was built in 1947 with a "binuclear" plan and flaring, butterfly roofs.)

For his work on the Geller House II, Rob's father won the prestigious Builder of the Year award, from the National Association of Home Builders. Young Rob was able to visit the construction site and meet Breuer in person. Both the house and the architect made a lasting impression. The broad expanses of glass and long-span arches of the vaulted concrete roof allowed for an open and uninterrupted flow, breaking down conventional hierarchies of inside versus outside; between living, kitchen, dining, and bedrooms; and between public and private spaces. Compared to his father's other projects, the Geller House was all about liberation—both spatial and social—and even seventeen-year-old Rob could understand this in the most visceral ways imaginable. He could feel it in his bones.

Ongoing conflicts between father and son—design versus build, traditional versus experimental, would, in many ways, shape Rob's career and future design philosophy. These opposing forces also gave him an edge, something to push against—both in the ways of rebellion and conformity, of fitting in while standing out—and would eventually lead to his own independent style of work.

Barnes and Coy consolidated their lifelong friendship at Portsmouth Priory in Portsmouth, Rhode Island, a Roman Catholic boarding school for boys, strictly run, where students were taught by English Benedictine monks and required to attend mass at 6 a.m. They both took a course in the sixth form called Art & Civilization (A&C) that was taught by Father Hillary, a charismatic teacher and housemaster. The class was only open to eight seniors at a time, and they had to be invited by the father. As a Benedictine monk, he had taken the vow of poverty but had come from a highly cultured family of means and social connections.

"Father Hillary had entrée to everything," said Coy, who remembered going to the Frick Collection with Hillary on days when the museum was closed to the public. In his slide lectures, Father Hillary would show his A&C students how architecture and art were important parts of culture and would make unlikely connections between different periods of history—how, for instance, Le Corbusier's Sainte Marie de la Tourette Monastery of the 1950s had certain similarities to a building designed by Leonardo da Vinci in the fifteenth century.

In the spring of 1969, Father Hillary took his students to Washington, DC, to visit the National Gallery, just after it had reopened in a new building by I. M. Pei. He showed them the work of Giotto, Andrea del Sarto, and other Renaissance painters. "I remember him teaching us about Filippo Brunelleschi and his designs for Saint Peters," said Coy.

Barnes graduated from the Priory in 1968, and Coy finished the following year. In 1972, after studying at Georgetown University

opposite page: Koch House, Papagayo, Costa Rica.

for two years, Barnes transferred to Cornell University and entered the five-year program in architecture. At Cornell, he was influenced by Jett Wells, Mike Dennis, and Guillermo Jullian de la Fuente who had worked at Le Corbusier's office in Paris.

"Jullian de la Fuente was a man of few words but very thoughtful," recalled Barnes. "His thinking was like a labyrinth."

In 1975, Barnes attended summer school in Venice where he studied with Colin Rowe, the erudite English critic and architectural theorist, and Werner Seligmann, a German American architect.

Barnes graduated from Cornell in 1977 and launched his professional career by designing a few projects for his father, the first commission being a small house in the low-lying Beach Hampton area of Amagansett. "That's when I learned about scale," recalled Barnes.

Two years later, in 1979, Barnes started working for architect Norman Jaffe. Jaffe was at the peak of his form, having recently completed the much-publicized Krieger House in Montauk and the Lloyds House in East Hampton. At heart, Jaffe was a tried-and-true modernist, but he offered his clients an alternative to the cool, almost clinical modernism of the New York Five, in particular, the all-white houses of Richard Meier or the geometric fabrications of Charles Gwathmey, both of whom were competitors for East End commissions. Jaffe's was a more sensual romanticism that many preferred, with natural textures and materials, while employing forms that, still minimal in their geometries, suggested more comforting vernacular traditions—old barns and farmhouses—as with the Becker House in Wainscott and the Perlbinder House in Sagaponack.

Barnes had deep admiration for Jaffe's sometimes eccentric methodologies, and from Jaffe, he learned about the poetry of residential architecture. Barnes also learned about celebrating the beauty of the native East End landscape. He learned how to combine natural materials—rustic granite, grainy wood, hand-split cedar shingles—for dramatic effects and how to incorporate the area's sea-brewed light by saturating interiors with a combination of skylights and floor-to-ceiling windows. What started as a mentor-apprentice partnership soon grew into genuine friendship.

Among other Jaffe projects, Barnes designed a garage addition for the Stern House on Further Lane, East Hampton, and became project architect for the Martin Raynes House in Southampton with a broad sloping tiled roof. Barnes would work for Jaffe full-time over the next two years and grow quite close to the enigmatic, often impulsive architect who gained a reputation for his light-filled houses and a modernism that was sensual, tactile, and textured with natural materials.

Barnes learned many valuable lessons in Jaffe's office and not only about design, but just as importantly, how to deal with people. He learned the art of leading a client to understand one's architectural vision, of forging close alliances with both homeowners and construction crews. Jaffe was known to visit building sites and get physically involved in the process, hammering nails, helping move rocks into place for a terrace. After his experience with Jaffe, Barnes took a position in the office of Daniel Goldner Architects in New York, a young, Manhattan-based firm that had opened in 1980. He worked there for eighteen months before quitting and launching his own practice, designing homes for his father's construction company, and then on his own. While Barnes may have been committed to a modernist approach, the market on the East End was still predominantly for traditional forms of architecture.

After graduating from the Priory, Chris Coy attended Sarah Lawrence College in Bronxville, New York, where he majored in creative writing. He dropped out in 1971 to travel throughout Europe and work on his first novel while living in a small walk-up apartment at 7 Avenue Stephen Pichon across the street from L'École des Arts et Metiérs in Paris's 13th Arrondissement. The never-to-be-finished novel was called *The Razor* and was a semiautobiographical bildungsroman about a young man who rejects his parents' expectations and goes out to forge his own path in life.

After a year in Paris, Coy moved to the Canary Islands where he lived in a shepherd's cave overlooking the Playa del Toro Lagoon. "The place was still raw, before all the tourists came," said Coy, who remembers watching molten lava flowing down from the Cumbre Vieja volcano on the main island of La Palma. Coy shared the rent-free cave with a free-spirited twenty-five-year-old from New York. They caught fish with a spear gun and cooked them on a primitive stone fireplace that Coy built near the mouth of the cave. He would place freshly caught fish and potatoes on skewers and cook them in the fire. "It was very basic," said Coy, "but it worked."

He lived there for nine months and then moved to Amsterdam where he rented a converted canal barge owned by a Dutch architect. While holed up on the barge through the bitter winter of 1973, he read through the owner's extensive architecture library. The works of Wright and Le Corbusier made a particular impression as did a book about the work of the Dutch modernist Gerrit Rietveld. An early seed of inspiration had been planted.

By 1977, Coy had grown tired of living abroad and decided to return to the United States, and soon after became a real estate broker in the Hamptons, launching Devon Realty in 1981 and working out of a small building on Pantigo Road, East Hampton. During this same period (1981–85), Rob joined forces with Louis Burgdorf, a builder/carpenter he had met in Ithaca, New York, while studying at Cornell. Their design-build firm, Barnes & Burgdorf, completed several projects on Long Island, including a barnlike house for Larry Mohr, an attorney, on Hands Creek Road in East Hampton. There was a house for the Spanish artist Carlos Sansegundo at the Bell Estate, and a house built on an adjacent lot for Sandro Gemino, a show business impresario.

The Segundo House was composed of four wedge-shaped pavilions, all clad with cedar shingles and rotating around a small central courtyard. The design combined both modern and traditional sensibilities. Opposing butterfly roofs gave the house its name: La Mariposa—"butterfly" in English—suggesting the geometric purity of Charles Gwathmey's early work, while alluding to old barns and

vernacular saltbox houses. The Gemino House was a single-story, half octagon that surrounded a pool and terrace.

Barnes also designed a house on Arbor Path, in the same neighborhood, that was an homage to his former boss, Norman Jaffe, as it featured a pyramidal roof, similar to Jaffe's sweeping "sky houses" of the late 1970s in which a broad, sloping roof mass became the dominant design feature. Although it was originally built as a "spec" house, Rob's father bought it and lived there with his wife, Betty.

Although these early commissions showed a steep learning curve and layers of compromise, they gave Barnes an opportunity to test out ideas he had been developing since his student days at Cornell. While he tried to stay true to his modernist predispositions, it was the peak of the postmodern period when neo-traditionalism was sweeping the fields and dunes of eastern Long Island with new/old houses by Robert A. M. Stern, Jaquelin Robertson, and Francis Fleetwood, who popularized a form of the shingle style that signaled old-money status and social arrival.

Around this period, Barnes designed several houses in the preferred neo-traditional style, with pitched roofs, Palladian windows, and covered wrapround porches. These included a house on Highway Behind the Pond, East Hampton, for David Lazer, producer of the Muppets TV show, and another for the Regan family that was a gambrel-roofed mansion overlooking the Maidstone golf course. Both projects received a good deal of attention and raised Barnes's architectural profile, even if it was not exactly the message he wanted to send. This kind of conflict between convention and innovation would carry on throughout his career.

By 1989, there was a change in the air. Barnes began plans for the Stanley Arkin House to be built on a dramatic site overlooking Gardiners Bay. Barnes assumed that Arkin wanted something traditional, so he designed a shingle-style imitation of the old Bell Estate manor, but Arkin was not convinced and asked Barnes to come up with a modern design.

The revised plan carried some of the scale, proportions, and linearity of a traditional manor house, but one that was rendered in a pared-down style with flat roofs, broad sheaths of glass, and a cubistic kind of fracturing along the facade. Internal spaces were outwardly expressed in different materials—wood, stone, glass, stucco—and connected by a long transverse bridge supported by a massive steel truss. This bridgelike volume contained the main living spaces.

"It was a soul-destroying thing to do," said Coy, who had already grown bored with the Hamptons real estate business and often found himself wandering in and out of Barnes's design studio to talk about the latest project. This was when he began to seriously consider architecture as a possible career. Ever since Europe, Coy had been growing more and more interested in architecture. He had explored many historic buildings while in France, including the sixteenth-century Tour Saint-Jacques on Rue Rivoli, and the Grand Mosque across from the Jardin des Plantes, but had been especially intrigued by the Pantheon, the neoclassical mausoleum on Montagne

opposite page: Owen House, Palm Springs, California.

Sainte-Geneviève that had been designed by Jacques-Germain Soufflot. "There was something about the massing and the way the light came through the central dome that fascinated me," said Coy. "I kept walking around the perimeter of the building, trying to figure it out."

Then, in 1982, at the age of thirty-one, he made a sudden decision to enroll in a five-year Bachelor of Architecture program at the Spitzer School of Architecture at the City College of New York. Among other projects, Coy designed a performance barge with an amphitheater that would sail up and down the Hudson River. In one assignment, he developed a proposal for an artists' live-work project on Manhattan's West Side that incorporated a segment of the elevated freight rail line that later became the High Line.

In 1986, Coy completed his studies and started to work with Barnes in East Hampton. After a year, Coy moved back to Manhattan and took a position in the office of Gwathmey Siegel, at a time when that firm was designing an addition to the Solomon R. Guggenheim Museum. For most of his time there, Coy worked on the interiors of an 18,000-square-foot house outside of Austin, Texas, for Michael Dell.

A year later, in 1993, Coy decided to leave Gwathmey's office and join forces with Barnes, officially launching Barnes Coy Architects in eastern Long Island. Chris's wife, Joann, an illustrator, was pregnant when Chris and Rob agreed on the partnership. Joann gave birth to their daughter, Camille, on September 30, 1993, and they moved to the Hamptons in late November.

Over the next twenty-five years, the two architects would establish a synergistic collaboration drawn largely from their mutual interest in the modern movement, and an equally passionate love for the landscape and light of eastern Long Island. Together they developed a uniquely hybrid approach to architecture that was grounded in the iconic sources of twentieth-century design, from Frank Lloyd Wright to Mies van der Rohe, Le Corbusier, Alvar Aalto, and Marcel Breuer, with a particular emphasis on site, natural materials, surface texture, and light.

From the start, Barnes and Coy found themselves agreeing on a certain set of design principles that they would continue to hone and develop over the next twenty-five years: transparency, materiality, invention, integrity of structure, and originality of form mixed with an almost obsessive attention to detail. Barnes would often start with an idea about form, while Coy would focus on the site. They would meet at Bobby Van's in Bridgehampton, and scribble ideas on the paper tablecloth, often finishing each other's drawings. Coy's approach was usually to try out a new idea and take certain risks. Within the new partnership, Barnes became more willing to take those same kinds of risks, both in form as well as structure and material.

Although they would build a number of commercial projects over the years, the architects came to specialize in single-family residences, one-of-a-kind dream houses for affluent clients that expressed a casual and highly intimate relationship with sea, sky, and individual lifestyle. "A house contains all typologies," said Coy. "It contains shelter, elements of the sacred, personal history, the locus of one's family life. It's also a statement of who you are, your identity. It's a museum, a temple, a workplace, and basic shelter. Designing a house is the front line of architecture." Their houses would be minimal in form yet responsive to the native environment and immediate surroundings.

Although the majority of the firm's 250-plus projects are located on eastern Long Island, they have also built projects in California, Colorado, Georgia, Florida, Saint Barts, and Costa Rica. All of their work, whether in the Hamptons or elsewhere, has been grounded in the spirit of place and a poetic response to light, water, and the natural topography of the site.

Sometimes their plans are in response to a particular zoning issue or environmental restriction. The curving facade of an 11,000-square-foot house in Water Mill, New York, for instance, echoes the concave setback from wetlands that surround a small pond, while the opposite side of the house opens up to the ocean with hovering, boxlike bays that run parallel to the coastal erosion hazard line. It was as if the final shape of the house had been predetermined by the conditions of the site.

Their first major commission as a design team was a waterfront house for Stanley Diller, a mathematician and financial analyst who specialized in predicting stocks and economic trends. After almost losing the job for lack of realistic estimates, Coy and Barnes decided to build the house themselves. Although Barnes had some construction experience working for his father, it was still a financial risk to undertake a design-build commission at such an early point in their careers.

The house featured a sixty-foot-long glass wall looking out over Gardiners Bay from a high bluff at the Bell Estate in Amagansett. It was a bold and daring design, a highly engineered structure, working with an unlikely mixture of influences, from John Lautner and Frank Lloyd Wright to Charles Gwathmey and Mayan ruins. The foundation, columns, and supporting walls were made from a rugged Pennsylvania limestone that would become one of the firm's signature materials. The rugged stone foundation and columns resembled the remnants of an old fortress.

A cylindrical form, something like a farm silo, was clad with smooth teak siding and rose near the center of the composition in contrast to the rugged stone elements. (The silo contained a library with a fireplace, a guest bedroom, and the central staircase.) A sixty-foot-long Vierendeel-truss bridge crossed over a pool and a sunken terrace before leading into the main living-dining room, a soaring, semielliptical space with a sloping aileron roof clad in copper, and a curving, eighteen-foot-high curtain wall of glass that looked over Gardiners Bay.

"We realized that we were trying to achieve a clarity of expression by articulating the envelope, the glass enclosure, from the structure, keeping them apart and not letting them touch one another," said Coy. They didn't fully understand this until they had actually seen the completed house and it was clear what was enclosure versus what was structure. They found this level of clarity to be beautiful.

"It became a religion for us to articulate the envelope from the underlying bones," said Coy. "In the future, every one of our houses would have this negligee of transparency working in contrast to the muscularity of the structure."

When finished, in 1995, the Diller House received a good deal of attention. It was published in newspapers and design journals, and was featured on the cover of a book about contemporary stone houses: *Stone Built: Contemporary American Houses* by Lee Goff. It set the imprint for things to come and effectively put the firm on the map.

Although the Diller House led to other commissions, there were not that many clients willing to throw caution to the wind and allow this level of experimentation. The Hamptons were still under the spell of postmodern pastiche, and the kind of architectural statements that signaled arrival.

In 1997, they started work on a house in Vail, Colorado, for Peter Knobel, a real estate developer and telecommunications executive. The house was clad with rustic stone facing and was all about the mountain views. Working with the kind of bearing compass that sailors use, Coy climbed up on the roof of the existing house and lined up all the best views in the valley. At one point, he stepped backward and tumbled off the edge of the roof but luckily fell on a pile of firewood and wasn't injured.

Not all of the projects from this period were built on such dramatic sites. In 2000, Barnes Coy designed a relatively modest (1,900-square-foot) house for Stuart and Susan Silverman in a densely wooded part of East Hampton. The clients wanted a feeling of spatial serenity, as if the house were part of the surrounding landscape. "We tried to make it disappear into the wilderness of the Northwest Woods," said Barnes, who wanted to create the feeling of a Scandinavian retreat, where simple outdoor living took precedence over appearances. Although there are no ocean or mountain views, the architecture defines its own kind of territorial imperative as a well-organized enclave surrounded by trees.

Two cubelike volumes—one containing private family spaces, the other containing public spaces (living, kitchen, dining)—penetrate one another and intersect at a forty-five-degree angle. "The idea was to physically define what you can't see," said Coy. A bridgelike walkway leads from the parking area into a central foyer and the main living space that opens to woodland views through a twenty-four-by-twenty-four-foot window. The four bedrooms are contained within a smaller, opaque volume clad in horizontal bands of cedar. A flagstone terrace and lap pool extend out toward the forest. The variety of levels, volumes, angles, and surface treatments evokes the geometric modernism of early Charles Gwathmey and Richard Meier houses while creating the illusion of a bigger house.

opposite page: Susser House, East Hampton, New York.

LIQUIDITY
Oceanfront House

From the beach, looking up over the wavering line of dunes, the Oceanfront House resembles a classic modernist pavilion: flat-roofed, one story, and rectilinear in plan—think Mies van der Rohe or Marcel Breuer—and from such a distance, it appears to hover above the sandy terrain, buoyant and airy, its open plan bracketed within a white stucco superstructure interspersed with sheaths of hurricane-proof glass. When you come closer, the illusion dissolves and you can see that it's not a single-story pavilion after all, but a three-level structure with more than 11,000 square feet of living space, not floating but anchored to the flood-prone site on massive cast-concrete plinths.

A neo-traditional house from the 1980s originally sat on the site, but the clients and architects agreed that it should be demolished to make way for a new structure that was modern, more sustainable, and custom tailored to the clients' needs. "We started by climbing up on a ladder and taking photographs to determine the sight lines," said Coy. After close scrutiny of the natural environment and local building codes, the architects developed a master plan that responded, almost viscerally, to the topographic surveys and FEMA floodplain maps. "FEMA became our closest ally," said Coy.

After presenting the clients with several different schemes—including a V-shaped roof and lens-shaped floor plan—the architects and clients settled on a curving facade that mirrored the setback line of wetlands that surround a freshwater pond to the north, whereas the opposite side would open up to the Atlantic Ocean with hovering, boxlike bays that ran parallel to the coastal erosion line. Once the basic footprint had been established, it became an organic, self-organizing process with the intended goal of full immersion in the natural environment. During a painstakingly drawn-out design process, the overall form was filled in and then gradually eroded to become a kind of armature or skeletal scaffolding around which the various programmatic ingredients could be arranged. In the final design, the outer shell curves outward in some places while retracting in others.

There's an inherent sense of performance and spectacle in the architecture, a breezy transparency and restless shifting of planes, especially on the upper levels. Glass curtain walls on both the north and south facades are made up of six-foot-wide panels of flat, not curved, glass, as if the outer membrane had been peeled back to reveal the interior spaces in full disclosure. Even the floor plates are exposed behind faceted surfaces of glass. For privacy, the owners can lower mechanized blinds concealed within the ceilings.

opposite page: A pink, gel-coated dining table by Wendell Castle sets the stage for infinite ocean-front living.

pages 28–29: From the beach, the house appears as a single-story pavilion floating above the dunes.

pages 30–31: The dining/kitchen area flows out to the ocean horizon through a glass curtain wall.

page 32: Folded metal surface of the fireplace wall, fabricated in Italy by De Castelli, features vertical striations and channels of random width.

page 33: Cantilevered porches and ramps open out to the south, in celebration of sun, sea, and sky.

pages 34–35: White, hand-finished stucco walls offset the owners' collection of contemporary art. Art by Marilyn Minter.

pages 36–37: Interior details: a recessed handrail on the central staircase; steel-and-glass stringers on the back staircase.

pages 38–39: Stairs to the first floor and master bedroom with a view over the pond. Art (left to right): ©Richard Prince, Barbara Kruger, and Tom Wesselman.

Two girls meet on the beach at Miami. One says:
"So what's new?"
The other says, "Wait'll you hear! I was at the doctor's this morning, he gives me an examination, and you know what he says? He says I'm gradually turning into a man."
"So what else is new?"
is bought and sold?

The spatial heart of the design is a central staircase that rises up from the ground level like the chambers of a nautilus shell, creating a vertical nucleus to what is otherwise a horizontally splayed composition. As an artifact, the staircase has the purity of an Ellsworth Kelly sculpture, and gives a nuanced order to the rest of the house. The open treads were made from thick slabs of white oak, while stringers and railings were made from curved panels of 5/8-inch-thick steel plate that were ground down to an ultrasmooth surface and finished with seven coats of sparkling white auto-body paint. One of the more elegant details is a recessed handrail that is illuminated from within by a strip of LED lighting—what Coy calls an "exercise in sensuality." Sections of the staircase were prefabricated at Tebbens Steel in Calverton, New York, and assembled on-site. A fritted-glass skylight casts light down through the elliptical openings, further emphasizing the staircase's complex geometries and shapely curves. The second-level spaces—guest rooms, children's bedrooms, and playroom—were too low to see over the dunes and catch full ocean views, so these rooms were oriented to views of the freshwater pond.

When you reach the third level, internal spaces expand laterally and explode out toward the Atlantic Ocean on one side and the pond on the other. A long, undulating table by Wendell Castle—something like a giant pink tongue—commands the open kitchen-dining area, as does a looping bentwood chandelier by John Procario that hangs above the table. A deeply furrowed chimney mass separates the main living area from a more private study. Light ripples across the vertical striations of the folded metal surface. (The fireplace was designed by Pembrooke & Ives in collaboration with the architects and was fabricated in Italy by De Castelli.) "We didn't want a regular pattern," said Coy. "It's more of a random sequence."

The eastern end of the house is more tightly clustered, the master bathroom being a boxlike entity framed in teak and bulging to the east like a Persian balcony, while the western end deconstructs itself with an open-faced framework that supports the pool terrace and an upper-level sky deck designed for sweeping views and family gatherings with its own kitchen, zinc bar, and Corten steel firepit.

The most dreamlike element is the transparent glass swimming pool, a high-concept fishbowl that acts as a liquid metaphor, mediating between ocean on one side and wetlands on the other, water to water. The pool is ten feet deep and is raised twenty feet above grade to capture ocean views. It holds more than a hundred tons of water. To avoid cracking, the pool has been reinforced with hefty concrete beams that extend fifty feet back into the structure of the house. The pool itself was made from mirrored glass with large, transparent "windows" facing west, south, and east, and makes for the most surreal moment of surprise when someone swims past the transparent opening and appears suspended in an aquamarine blue void.

The eastern side of the pool becomes the back wall of a parlor, where you can sit on a purple couch and gaze up through the pool, a most unusual sensation. "I wanted the water to appear solid, as if you were swimming through the room," said Coy. "It's a Dr. No moment."

pages 40–41: An 11,000-square-foot house features a transparent swimming pool projecting from second floor.

pages 42–43: View through the swimming pool from the second-floor study.

opposite page: Transparent wine storage at the end of the second-story hallway. Art by Allora & Calzadilla.

pages 46–47: Details of the pool and study.

pages 48–49: Entrance to the house seen from the west. The curving facade echoes the environmental set-back line.

See plans of the Oceanfront House on page 280.

WHEN IT COMES TO ART
HUMOR IS THE SADDEST STROKE
IT IS LIKE CRYING OUT DIDO'S LAMENT
"WHEN I AM LAID IN EARTH REMEMBER ME BUT AH! DON'T FORGET MY FATE"
- PURCELL
THEN I SNAP OUT OF IT
IN THE END I BELIEVE PICTURES SAY IT BETTER

COURTYARD

Meadow House

You approach down a long straight driveway shaded by Japanese Zelkova trees, and the drawn-out introduction creates a kind of cinematic suspense with wildly contrasting patches of light and shadow continuing throughout the grounds and into the house itself where there are pools of light within pools of light. It's like the opening sequence of a 1930s Hollywood movie. The clients purchased the four-acre property twenty-five years earlier, but the preexisting house suffered from serious drainage problems and the basement often flooded with rainwater. After lengthy discussions, they decided to tear down the old house and build something new and dry.

They had been looking at Belgian farmhouses and other traditional kinds of domestic architecture, so Barnes Coy presented a model with a Flemish hipped roof and another that looked like a Napa Valley winery house, but eventually they were able to make the case for a thoroughly modern house with flat roofs and floor-to-ceiling glass that would not only be more appropriate for the site but better suited to their programmatic needs: the clients wanted five bedrooms and a big kitchen. They wanted a sense of the outside coming inside and every room to be flooded by natural light. They also needed ample wall space to hang a substantial collection of contemporary art.

Unlike Barnes Coy's outward-directed beach houses, this was not going to be another "view house," but more of a hivelike composition with internally organized circulation and light filtering in from every side, a garden courtyard at the center and ground-floor rooms placed around the periphery in low, "ground-scraping" symmetry. Wanting a bold statement at the point of entry, the architects proposed a wall of rusting Corten steel, like a Richard Serra sculpture, but the steel would be difficult to maintain, so instead, the entry wall was fabricated with ceramic panels in a rust-red glaze, as close to the color of rusting steel as could be matched. It makes for a psychological barrier, as if it were the vestige of a walled encampment.

One enters the inner sanctum on a raised teak boardwalk and through a ten-foot-wide opening in the ceramic wall, into a forecourt that's landscaped like a miniature park of semicontrolled wilderness. Rough flagstones, left over from the original house, were used to create a cross-axial pathway that leads to glass doorways on either side. Liriope grass was used as ground cover while crepe myrtle trees provide privacy. Two thirteen-foot-deep light wells are surrounded by low barriers of steel and densely tufted fountain grass. The light wells illuminate a subterranean level with recreation room, gym, guest rooms, and media theater.

opposite page: Light-filled gallery surrounds the inner courtyard. Paintings by Sean Landers.

pages 52–53: The central walkway runs through an opening in a rust-colored ceramic wall and into the lushly landscaped courtyard.

pages 54–55: The main axis leads into a spacious living room with travertine marble hearth. Sculpture on right by Lorin Marsh.

pages 56–57: Details of the staircase to the second floor with glass railings. Painting by Nicolas Party.

pages 58–59: A counter separates the kitchen from the family living area, which is illuminated by a sculptural lighting fixture.

pages 60–61: The family room and breakfast area look out onto the courtyard garden.

The axial line of approach continues through the main entrance and into the central living room, finally terminating in a symbolic fashion at a twenty-foot-high hearth of travertine marble. All interior furnishings and decorative objects are from Lorin Marsh, the design showroom of Caryn Schacht, one of the homeowners. A sun-drenched gallery wraps around the periphery of the main courtyard. Two other guest rooms and the daughter's bedroom are strung along its eastern side, while to the west is a large kitchen with an informal dining area, and a guest suite with its own walled-in courtyard. The only section that rises above the one-story height is the master bedroom suite, a blocklike extrusion of pale gray cedar that pokes up like a captain's wheelhouse.

The 8,000-square-foot house opens to the back of the four-acre property through a formal dining room, library, and living room, which has twelve-foot-high windows that look out over the parklike landscape. The original entry to the property faced west, so the architects' first move was to rotate the direction to a north-south axis, which changed the spatial organization of the design. An existing tennis court was left in the northwest corner of the property, but they got rid of a small guesthouse as well as the original swimming pool that was replaced with a long lap pool running north to south along the western side of the property.

Chris LaGuardia, landscape architect, created a parterre in the back of the house with perennial borders and a mix of Russian sage, salvia, asters, and wild grasses, "like a designed meadow," said LaGuardia, who shaped the ground plane into widely spaced turf steps that are held in place by Corten steel risers, and lead up to a wilder, less structured garden. Select plants, like a group of old willows and a large katsura tree, were preserved or relocated. A venerable copper beech, growing in the middle of the property, was moved a hundred feet to the east so that it would anchor the northeast end of the house and provide a generous canopy of shade, while a long allée of honey locust trees was planted to create a walkway to the back of the property where the clients host large summer parties.

page 62: Steps down from the steel pergola to the pool terrace at the northwest corner courtyard garden.

page 63: An informal dining area looks out to the terrace.

pages 64–65: Floating planes of the house carry into the "designed meadow."

opposite page: Master bathroom.

pages 68–69: A guest room looks out to a private garden courtyard. Painting by Fredrik Vaerslev.

pages 70–71: A raised teak boardwalk leads through the entry of the garden planted with wild grasses and crepe myrtle trees.

See plans of the Meadow House on page 280.

TRANSPARENCY

Koch House I

Even though the two-story Koch House has more than 6,000 square feet of living space—much of it hidden below grade—it appears to be a smaller, self-contained pavilion in the mid-century spirit of architects like Peter Blake, George Nelson, and Andrew Geller. But in this case, nothing has been sacrificed in the way of comfort or modern necessities, nor was privacy a serious consideration as the house is surrounded by ten pastoral acres of green. The immediate grounds are planted with native trees, and there's a large pond that further buffers the eastern side of the property. "The fact that it's a totally private area enabled us to make it almost entirely out of glass," said Coy. The only opaque section on the otherwise transparent facade is a two-story wall of Burmese teak that was laid in horizontal planks. It screens a ground-floor powder room and the elevator shaft. The teak was left untreated, which allowed it to weather to a driftwood gray.

It's very much a boxlike object sitting on its flat, tablelike surface and the inherent boxiness is further affirmed by the way the eastern end appears to hang off a decline in grade. It's a sleight of hand—the foundation has been blacked out to read as void—but achieves the desired effect of a house surfing the landscape. Furthermore, the stucco fascia wraps around the exterior as a continuous white ribbon, defining the corners, foundation, and roof plane while concealing a steel superstructure that supports the weight of the house and allows such a lighter-than-air illusion. Structurally, there are ten-by-ten-inch crossbars that prevent lateral movement, while the glass curtain wall is supported by strident aluminum mullions, two inches wide, that also carry part of the load.

It's as if a screen had been pulled back to reveal the internal logic of the house so that it reads like an abstract painting, a three dimensional Mondrian with all of the essentials exposed. The test-tube effect is particularly effective in the early evening hours when the house is backlit by the setting sun and everything stands out in high relief. Even the furniture—a butterfly chair, a custom-designed couch, a Corbusier-Perriand chaise—take on star status in the amber glow.

Out front, parallel bars of cast concrete (eighteen inches wide by six feet long) have been recessed into the lawn to make a subtly restrained, low-impact walkway that leads from the parking area to the main entrance. This simple gesture establishes a central axis as well as a proportion based on the human stride that carries throughout the architecture. From the walkway, the zigzag pattern of the staircase is showcased through a curtain wall of glass and energizes the entire composition with an almost transcendent quality, airy and graceful

opposite page: Two sections of the 6,000-square-foot plan are attached by a raised deck and underground passageway.

pages 74–75: Twin volumes are set in perpendicular relationship and surrounded by ten acres of agricultural preserve.

pages 76–77: The interior perch cantilevers over the twenty-two-foot-high void of the living-dining area. Painting by Andrea Bischof.

yet muscular, while it appears to defy gravity, strengthened by an invisible glass railing slotted into the stringers to provide more structural integrity. The treads are three-inch-thick slabs of teak, while the stringers are hollow tubes of black steel welded together in a chevron pattern.

The entire floor deck on the second level is set back a foot from the perimeter walls to reinforce the hovering, glass-box illusion. A small, second-floor seating area (what Barnes Coy refer to as the "tongue") cantilevers out above the twenty-two-foot-high void of the dining-living area below. The upstairs level also features the master bedroom, dressing rooms, and a private living room. A central bay projects out from the rear facade and encloses identical his-and-her office spaces that are separated by an open-riser staircase leading to a rooftop deck. Climbing up this high, recessed staircase—something like a geologic fissure—feels like the conclusion of a well-tempered sequence that started in the parking lot and continued through a series of spatial folds until it ends here, on the roof-deck. The rest is all sky and views out over the agricultural preserve. From such an elevated vantage, one looks down to a black granite infinity pool with a waterfall splashing into a large, twenty-person spa. The pool area is surrounded by a recessed moat, a modern-day ha-ha, two feet deep, six feet wide, and planted with Russian sage so as to provide the required safety barrier while allowing unobstructed views to the back of the property. Deep within the capacious basement level, there's a recreation room, cold-plunge pool, workout gym, family movie theater, bedroom for the live-in chef, as well as a laundry room, multicar garage, and a subterranean passageway that leads to the guesthouse, a scaled-down version of the main house that plays counterpoint to the larger volume while mirroring its shape, structure, and surface textures.

Michael Blake, a landscape architect who specializes in sustainable design, wanted to create the feeling of natural wildness without self-conscious design strategies while respecting the minimal lines of the Barnes Coy architecture and the legacy of Sagaponack's open farm fields. He preserved existing cedars and privet that shade the 150-foot-long driveway but removed a cluster of old maples that were blocking views. He screened the western boundary with a grove of river birches, used crepe myrtles on the eastern side, and planted rows of cryptomeria (Japanese cedar) to help mitigate wind and block out neighboring houses. The north end of the lawn tapers off into a border of wild grasses and beyond that, the homeowners installed a full-size soccer field for their sons. Beyond the soccer field lies a fifty-acre tract of protected farmland.

opposite page: The staircase is made from three-inch-thick slabs of teak, steel stringers, and glass safety railings.

pages 80–81: A sectional couch creates a defined living area on the ground floor.

STUDIO KO

opposite page: The eastern end of the house appears to project out over a decline in grade. Photo by Paul Domzal.

above: The guesthouse is attached to the main house by a raised deck and underground passageway.

pages 84–85: (Left) A guesthouse window. (Center) Six-foot-long bars of cast concrete create a walkway to the front entrance while echoing the Burmese teak brise-soleil (right) on the front facade.

pages 86–87: The house maintains an object-like purity as it rides above the sprawling, ten-acre site.

See plans of the Koch House I on page 281.

MARSHLAND

Bayfront House

opposite page: A street facade as an abstract collage of different textures: shingles, smooth cedar siding, and Bendheim Channel glass panels.

pages 90–91: A tidal marsh, part of a fifty-acre nature preserve, stretches to the west of the property.

page 92: Teak treads and a glass safety railing for the floating staircase.

page 93: Recessed openings for the garage door and skylight cut into the taut shingled surface.

page 94: A slitlike opening commands a view of the tidal marsh and beach.

page 95: A second-floor deck opens out from the casual family living area.

pages 96–97: Details and subtle gradations of material and surface texture.

page 98: A guest bedroom with a hanging bubble chair by Eero Aarnio.

page 99: The master bathroom suite illuminated by translucent glass panels.

pages 100–101: Every interior space defers to the natural setting of the freshwater creeks, sandy beach, and osprey nests.

See plans of the Bayfront House on page 281.

The twisting and shifting is due, in large part, to the fact that the lot is essentially a triangle while the house has four sides. "We had to work with this tricorn-hat envelope with setbacks on all sides," said Coy. "It made for a kind of fractalated geometry that suggested interlocking triangles." Each side of the house addresses a different site condition and environmental ordinance: tidal wetlands to the west, anxious neighbors to the east, sandy beach to the south, roadway to the north. The composition was pulled and twisted in a way that reflected all of these conflicting forces.

The street-side facade is an intricately balanced composition, a study in values, with subtle gradations in tone, degrees of transparency, and surface tension—from roughly split shingles to the ruggedly finished granite of the foundation, to smoothly weathered cedar on the garage door and entry porch. Six windows, of different shapes and sizes punch through the tautly stretched outer skin. Some of the windows protrude, others are recessed; translucent panels of Bendheim Channel glass create a sliding, shoji-screen effect. "We wanted contrasting textures," said Coy. "We liked the way the shingles returned into the deep recesses. They're very tactile and luxurious to the eye." While the vocabulary is essentially modern, the shingle siding and window treatment suggest a concession to local vernacular traditions, as does the way the house is locked into a tight, orthogonal relationship with the street, which is set back about twenty feet and running parallel with New Suffolk Avenue.

The architecture redefines itself as it turns the corner and erupts. All historical associations quickly vanish as the flatness and rectilinear purity of the front facade dissolve into triangular planes and partitions that splay toward the south to capture views of Peconic Bay, Robins Island, and the South Shore, while turning away from an obtrusive neighbor to the east. The outer surface shifts from rough shingles to smoothly milled cedar siding that wraps around the waterside like an elastic ribbon. The small openings of the front give way to broad expanses of glass and a narrow observation that looks out to the south.

The site's greatest asset, however, is the saltwater marsh that stretches immediately to the west. Virtually every architectural space defers to this natural spectacle, a tidal ecosystem of watery meadows, cordgrass, silverweed, and spike-grass interlaced with freshwater creeks, sandy shoals, and brackish pools. While the main living area of the house is equipped with a television screen and fireplace, the principal form of family entertainment is gazing through the floor-to-ceiling glass at the ever-changing play of light and shadow across the surface of the marsh. The fifty-acre preserve—and former site of a Corchaug Tribe settlement—provides habitat for all manner of fish and wading birds (herons, egrets, sandpipers), but the airways are ruled by a family of osprey who built its nest on top of a pylon directly in front of the house.

INVERSION

Susser House

The architects broke the 8,500-square-foot house down into three separate pavilions that are attached by an elongated breezeway on the north side, almost as if three smaller beach houses—each with its own distinctive character—had been joined at the hip. The final composition doesn't express a uniform oneness so much as a diverse "village" of parts, appearing from afar as disconnected but deeply integrated from within by connective passageways and staircases. "We wanted to break up the massing," said Coy. "Scale was an issue from the start."

There was an older house on the property that had little architectural merit—"a Mediterranean nightmare"—that was torn down to make way for the new house. In order to maximize ocean frontage and capture as many views as possible, the architects made it as long as local zoning laws allowed. It ended up being just over 140 feet in length, about half a football field. The east and west ends stretch right up to the setback lines on either side.

A straight line of bayberry, an allée of Chinese elm, and a rectangle of lawn run along the north side of the house to further emphasize the linearity of the facade and establish a more formal, ceremonial approach to the entry side of the property.

Although the architecture borrows from the mid-century beach-house vernacular of Peter Blake and George Nelson while emphasizing the inherent virtues of pure geometric form, sculptural integrity, and a one-to-one relationship with the natural setting, it's a thoroughly twenty-first-century interpretation. The conventional hierarchies of domestic space have been reassembled with a broader, post-digital range of spatial possibilities with a theatrical play of light versus shadow, revealing and concealing, as if orchestrated. Opaque surfaces—teak, stucco, granite, and zinc—alternate with transparent swaths of tempered glass.

The overall shape is a clamshell curving up toward the ocean with the western end bending slightly to the north, offering entry through a twenty-two-foot-high curtain wall that, in turn, leads to an atrium with an elevator and floating staircase. The high, angular atrium is further animated by a custom-designed light fixture by Andrea Claire Studio that dangles over the space like a Calder mobile with yellow, black, and white polyhedrons connected by steel rods.

This introductory section is the most compressed of the three pavilions, something like a fractured cube with diagonal skylights. In order to contain three bedrooms for children, a recreation room, guest rooms, and a three-car garage, the ceilings are only nine feet high compared to the soaring, twenty-two-foot ceilings in the central pavilion.

opposite page: A dominant feature of the interior is an inverted teak pyramid that hangs to within nine feet of the living-room floor. Painting by Jules Olitski.

pages 104–105: A sculptural play of geometric volumes and surface treatments: stucco, horizontal cedar siding, and stone interspersed with glass. Photo by Paul Domzal.

pages 106–107: A row of Chinese Elms and a stone foundation emphasize the linearity of the inland facade. (Landscape is by the LaGuardia Design Group.)

page 108: Glass facade with a view to the orchard.

page 109: A light-saturated gallery to the dining-kitchen area. Painting by Kenneth Noland.

page 110: (Left) Foyer staircase. (Right) Foyer with painting by Manolo Valdés.

page 111: (Left) Sculpture by Tom Otterness above entry foyer. (Right) Ceiling detail.

pages 112–113: Matching slabs of marble as a backsplash in the kitchen. Painting by Friedrich Kunath.

The local building code allows for a thirty-two-foot height if a house has a pitched roof but only a twenty-five-foot height if it has a flat roof. Without stating it in so many words, the code favors a more traditional style of architecture. The architects wanted the glass walls of their central pavilion to be at least twenty-two feet high. If they used a conventional pitch, they would be allowed to go to the desired height. They didn't want a traditional house with a peaked roof, however, and managed to sneak around the restrictions by concocting an inverted pyramid roof that technically followed the letter of the law. No one had ever proposed anything like it before. After some grumbling, the building department relented and allowed the roof to be thirty-two feet above natural grade.

"In the end, they had to grant us the permit," said Coy, who saw the outcome as a small victory over mediocrity. The "V" of the inverted roof points downward and inward like a directional marker, while making a distinctive profile that draws the eye toward the center of the composition. The sloping roof planes are clad in a muted, pewter-colored zinc in contrast to the walls of white stucco. (Zinc is one of the sturdiest and most salt-resistant materials for oceanfront conditions.)

Inside, the roof becomes an upside-down teak pyramid that hovers above the center of the living room while dropping down to within nine feet of the floor. As a presence, it is both monolithic and benign. Pressing down from above, it draws the eye upward and outward through high, triangular clerestory windows that saturate the living room with a subaqueous glow. Passing clouds and seagulls are framed within the 360-degree panorama.

The eastern pavilion features a mono-pitched roof that's also clad in zinc and contains the master bedroom suite with a double story space above and a fully equipped gym below. It's the most discretely objectlike of all the structures with white stucco walls and teak louvers for blocking the sun.

While the inland side of the property is highly organized and quite formal, the ocean side is much looser and nonlinear. An eccentrically shaped deck and swimming pool dip south and then angle back to the north, following the coastal erosion line. (You're allowed to build right up to the designated line.) The angular pool is surrounded by a recessed overflow trough and merges seamlessly with the oceanfront grounds that were left as wild as possible with the addition of bayberry and some other salt-resistant shrubs. The dune itself was restored and stabilized with native beach grass to help mitigate erosion, while California privet and Torulosa Juniper were used along the east and west boundaries for privacy and to mitigate prevailing winds.

page 114: The main living room looks out to dunes and ocean through a twenty-two-foot-high curtain wall.

page 115: A dynamic intersection of architectural elements at the pool terrace: curving cedar fascia, angled stone chimney, and glass prism. Photo by Paul Domzal.

pages 116–117: The angular form of the zero-edge infinity pool echoes the coastal erosion line and compliments the natural landscape of the dune grass and bayberry beyond.

page 118: The master bedroom enjoys an uninterrupted corner view of the oceanfront landscape. Painting by Richard Pousette-Dart.

page 119: The ceiling of the master bedroom features an inverted teak pyramid. Painting by Richard Pousette-Dart.

opposite page: Master bathroom.

pages 122–123: View of the house's restless volumes, as if a series of smaller beach houses had been joined together. Photo by Paul Domzal.

See plans of the Susser House on page 282.

BOW TIE

Gelfond House

For Barnes Coy Architects, the project turned into a willful act of compression: making a 5,280-square-foot house feel like an 8,000-square-foot house with six bedrooms, which was the client's desired program. The half-acre lot didn't allow for anything larger. It's set within a wild landscape of wind-stunted pines, dune grass, and bayberry, lying east of Amagansett, toward Napeague and Hither Hills, in a sandy, low-lying area that used to be called Beach Hampton. Building lots, originally laid out in the 1930s, are modest. Compared to the older bungalows in this beachfront community, this is a relatively large house, but miniscule in comparison with the recent crop of Hamptons trophy houses.

There was a preexisting structure: a small, undistinguished house from the 1970s, that sat right at the top of the dune. Local zoning forbade expansion of the footprint, so the old house was demolished, and the new structure was set back sixty-five feet from the dune and twenty-two feet from the road, as required by law. This made for a tightly prescribed building envelope, but it also gave the architects a starting point. The final design was yet another by-product of the designated zoning envelope that compelled the architects to work within an environmentally sustainable program, returning to the low-impact spirit of the postwar era when small, modernist beach houses by Peter Blake and Andrew Geller celebrated the innocent pleasures of summer living. It could even be seen as a radical statement in today's economic climate—not that 5,000 square feet is exactly a shack—but you don't need 30,000 square feet to enjoy the natural wonders of eastern Long Island or the simple joys of beachfront living.

The architects call it the "Bow Tie House" because the floor plan is pinched in the middle and flares out at either end, west to east, but to be accurate, it's actually two bow ties stacked asymmetrically on top of each other: one bow tie being black, the other being a pale wood color. The lighter of the two is clad in horizontal slats of naturally treated cedar. The darker volume is vertically clad in charred shou-sugi-ban cedar, a traditional Japanese method of sealing wood to prevent weathering. (Shou-sugi-ban siding comes with a thirty-year guarantee.) The blackened walls act as a shadowlike background to offset the lighter walls. While the inwardly angled "bow tie" facades echo the contours of the site, they also channel views out toward the water and away from neighboring houses. The ground-level terrace is made from Dekton porcelain slabs and reaches out to the coastal erosionline as it wraps around an angular, sixty-eight-foot-long swimming pool.

opposite page: The process of cutting and carving creates a sense of lateral movement as if one part were sliding through another. The windows are recessed, tilted or projected outward like angular extrusions. Photo by Paul Domzal.

pages 127–128: A thirty-eight-foot-wide balcony hangs over a porcelain-tiled terrace; the sixty-eight-foot-long lap pool follows the Coastal Erosion setback line. Photo by Paul Domzal.

The salt-and-pepper volumes penetrate each other in horizontal directions with the black portion defining the ground floor and the pale portion defining the upper. They also overlap and penetrate each other in a vertical relationship: the black rising up at the western end of the house, the pale dipping down to emphasize the street-side entry, while a central chimney mass rises up through the narrow "waist" of the house and helps anchor the colliding bow tie geometries.

It all makes for an interlacing of forms, pushing and pulling, compressing or releasing tension, and making the house feel lighter and less static. Even the windows are used as discretely positioned facets, recessed, tilted, or projecting outward like angular extrusions. This process of cutting and carving creates lateral movement, almost as if one part of the house were sliding through the other. A low, cubic mass of blackened cedar—a kind of vestigial tail—appears to pull away from the eastern end and rotate off axis. This section contains the living/media room as well as a guest room and pool cabana.

The steel-framed structure is anchored to the shifting, hurricane-prone site on a twelve-inch-thick bed of concrete. As a result, the interior spaces are able to flow freely from front to back, unencumbered by load-bearing walls or an excess of columns. (More than 190 tons of steel were used in the house's framework.) Nature pours in from every angle, through terraces, roof-decks, and six-foot-wide panels of hurricane-proof glass that wrap around the ocean side of the house. More than 30 percent of energy needs are provided by solar panels on the roof and the nine geothermal wells that were drilled three hundred feet belowground.

Interior spaces are not deeply recessed in the crisscrossing plan but thrust outward and defer to the natural environment. Every room has a special view, and the views are complemented by a neutral palette and pale, simple furnishings. All flooring and millwork are made from Spessart, a type of white oak from Bavaria. Bathroom walls, floors, and sinks were made from Bianco Dolomite, a white marble tile imported from Italy, while the central chimney mass was clad in pale Madras sandstone from India.

A hovering staircase with slablike treads of white oak rises from the light-suffused foyer and ascends to the main living-dining area, which was placed on the upper level, along with the master bedroom and kids' bedrooms, high enough to capture ocean breezes and views over the top of the primary dune. From here, a narrow set of four-inch-thick teak treads leads up to a roof-deck made from Brazilian ipe.

pages 126–127: 38-foot-wide balcony hangs over porcelain-tiled terrace; 68-foot-long lap pool follows Coastal Erosion setback line.

opposite page: Cantilevered teak treads behind glass wall lead from second-floor living area to roof deck.

page 130: Details: interpenetration of forms and stacked volumes.

page 131: Stairwell with light fixture and safety railings made from panels of ¾-inch laminated glass.

pages 132–133: Plan of "Bow tie House" is pinched in middle and flares out at either end; black volume is clad in charred shou-sugi-ban siding, paler volume in natural cedar siding. Photo by Paul Domzal.

See plans of the Gelfond House on page 282.

HARBOR

Beckenstein/O'Rourke House

"The best architecture is a kind of collaboration," said Arthur Beckenstein, a graphic designer who along with his husband, John O'Rourke, worked closely with a design team that included Barnes Coy, landscape architect Thomas Woltz (of Nelson Byrd Woltz), and interior designer Julia Roth. It's a densely choreographed arrangement on a 1.5-acre site that drops down from Oyster Shores Road toward Three Mile Harbor in East Hampton.

Beckenstein bought the property in 1976, and there was an undistinguished house from the 1950s already on the site. It was torn down to make way for the new construction, but because of local zoning laws, the architects were compelled to work within the dimensions of the preexisting footprint so that the faint ghost of a neo-traditional house lies buried within the DNA of the modern layout. Only the two-car garage remains intact from the older house, but other vestiges can still be sensed in the staggered entry sequence and the boxlike volumes of the new, 6,000-square-foot house that suggest the ghostly outlines of other rooms, unseen.

There's a natural spring that runs through the property and drains into the harbor at the bottom of the bluff. It was a watering hole for the local Montaukett tribe who called the area "Turtle Back" because of the shape of the land. House and grounds are linked by a neatly ordered sequence of parterres, flagstone terraces, grassy tiers, walkways, and walled gardens that reach out from the house and extend into the surrounding terrain, as if the descending levels were filters for the spring waters that spout naturally from the ground and gave the area its modern name: "Springy Banks."

Architecture merges with exterior landscape elements. A turret-shaped terrace of rugged fieldstone anchors the architecture into the sloping terrain at the southeastern corner. A footpath meanders through beds of liriope and Japanese pachysandra beneath a Chinese maple and down to the water's edge. A horizontal trellis runs along a sidewall and supports climbing hydrangea. Freestanding concrete walls rise like remnants of a ruin, along the western and northern sides of the pool, suggesting the outlines of the original house and extending the architecture even further into the landscape. One wall holds back the descending grade of earth, while the other frames a rectangular view of an adjacent gully that's been left naturally wild. Water gushes out of a dozen slitlike openings in the concrete wall and splashes into the pool, but reads more like a natural percolation, symbolic of the artesian springs that characterize this area. Above the swimming pool, there's an allée of crepe myrtle trees bordered by ferns. Earth and plants are held in place by a Corten steel retaining wall, a semiformal gesture

opposite page: The house is perched above a natural spring and looks out over the harbor.

pages 136–137: Architectonic volumes of stucco, glass, and fieldstone merge seamlessly with the exterior landscape.

pages 138–139: The living room looks out to an enclosed garden with the pool on one side and the harbor on other side. Interior furnishings are a mix of modern and rustic. Painting by Hector Leonardi.

that establishes an axis of movement along the western edge of the property. The slender trunks of the myrtles are mottled with silver and umber bark and, in autumn, the leaves turn a shimmering shade of yellow. From here, a matching Corten steel gateway leads back out to the parking area and street.

At the heart of the interior plan is the two-story void that leads from the main entrance aglow with light from the twenty-two-foot-high curtain wall that angles along the western facade. This wedge-shaped foyer tapers down to a narrow termination at its far end, creating the illusion of expanded depth. It's a kind of false perspective. All lines converge—mullions, horizontal slats of wood, stainless steel railings—drawing the eye both inward and outward at the same time: inward toward the living room; outward toward the garden terrace. The staircase rises from this same foyer as a kind of free-floating sculptural entity, an intricately detailed household god that's fabricated with maple treads and stainless steel railings.

Cranking the mezzanine back at an angle creates a deep well of light that streams in from three different directions (west, north, and south) through the wraparound wall of glass. "The house becomes a crystal cube that reflects the sky and trees," said Barnes. "If you're inside, it's fully transparent." The shape of the entry space mirrors, almost exactly, the trapezoidal swimming pool that lies to the west, and makes for a type of symmetry that registers in subtle, visceral ways as one moves through the rooms and senses similarly parallel spaces.

The main living room is essentially a breezeway between pool and harbor, fully saturated with liquid light reflecting off the two bodies of water, while highlighting an eclectic collection of art and furniture that combines modern and archaic elements: primitive millstones from Africa; a Mies van der Rohe bench, rice-paper lamps, a hand-carved throne from Ethiopia, a nubby woven rug, and a slab of glass resting on a gnarled piece of driftwood for a coffee table.

The fireplace mass is encased with ipe hardwood that creates a warmly textured surface as it divides living from dining areas and a professional kitchen equipped with translucent cabinets and zinc countertops. What started out as an opaque backsplash turned into a long, slitlike window that runs the breadth of the kitchen and opens it to water views.

The second-floor library is a private sanctuary that features color studies by Josef Albers, and built-in cabinetry by Corey Springer of Wüd Furniture Design, who also fabricated the library's bronze countertops and blackened-steel bookshelves. This quiet perch looks out over the poolside garden and a thick pelt of sedum—the leafy succulent—that covers the roof of the one-story garage and provides a natural form of insulation. Depending on the season, the sedum changes in hue from pale green to a deep russet red. Just behind the library lies the master bedroom suite with a deck overlooking Three Mile Harbor. The bedroom features a Chifruda winged chair by Sergio Rodrigues, and above the king-size bed, a twelve-foot-wide triptych of roaring ocean waves that homeowner Beckenstein photographed during Hurricane Hermine in 2016.

opposite page: The mezzanine level is angled back from the curtain wall to create a well of natural light. Painting by Hector Leonardi.

pages 142–143: The trapezoidal pool was designed as a garden folly with concrete retaining walls and gurgling fountains.

page 144: (Above) A transparent backsplash in the kitchen looks out to the garden. (Below) A zinc table and ipe walls in the kitchen-dining area. Painting by Andres Vidal.

page 145: (Above) The south façade seen from the garden. (Below) the master bedroom with a view over the harbor.

pages 146–147: A modernist staircase with stainless steel railings and floating treads is complimented by a carved Senufo hornbill from the Ivory Coast.

pages 148–149: The upper library level looks out over the pool and sedum-planted roof. Two studies by Josef Albers.

pages 150–151: Conspicuous patterns repeat while integrating architecture and landscape.

pages 152–153: The eastern facade overlooks the harbor with a cantilevered porch off the master bedroom.

See plans of the Beckenstein/O'Rourke house on page 283.

BROWN
ALE

CLIFFTOP
Segrete/Sack House

opposite page: A glassed-in breezeway between the private and public volumes.

pages 156–157: A floating staircase accentuates the east end of the open-plan living/dining/kitchen area.

page 158: An open stairwell with a view over Long Island Sound. Painting by Stefan Knapp.

page 159: An exterior steel staircase leads to the roof deck.

pages 160–161: Details of the interiors reflect the modern taste of the homeowners. Painting by Bret Webster.

page 162: A window wraps around a cedar-clad corner and overlooks the Long Island Sound.

page 163: The master bathroom off the editing studio. Photograph of John Lennon by Bob Gruen.

page 164: Pool and lawn at the top of the cliff.

page 165: The house sits on a clifftop fifty-five feet above the beach. Photo by Paul Domzal.

See plans of the Segrete/Sack House on page 283.

By employing a tripartite combination of materials, textures, and interpenetrating volumes, Barnes Coy created a design that appears larger and more complex than its actual square footage would indicate. The house was conceived as a year-round base where the clients could both live and work. (Segrete is an interior designer and event planner. Sack is a film and television editor.) From the village of Cutchogue, it's more than two miles to the north, through a stretch of sod farms. It's hard to imagine that there's still this much open land left anywhere on eastern Long Island.

The road ends in a cul-de-sac near a steep bluff that drops down to Long Island Sound. While it may stand out for its experimental design, the house fits in surprisingly well in the neighborhood of small, suburban-type houses, ranch and Cape Cod specials, built in the 1950s and 1960s. When it came to the design, the site was everything. The house sits fifty-five feet above sea level and is positioned squarely in the center of the lot to address the street while also capturing dramatic water views to the north and west. The lawn rolls gently to the edge of the bluff and then cascades down precipitously to the beach below.

Unlike many Barnes Coy houses, the budget of this commission was within a relatively modest range. Because of its size, the plan didn't call for a great deal of structural steel and the architects specified locally sourced materials wherever possible and off-the-shelf components like windows, sliding glass doors, and kitchen cabinetry in place of expensive, custom-made elements.

The 3,300-square-foot plan fits precisely within the prescribed building envelope with virtually nothing to spare. It's basically a cube on a cliff, but in this case, the cube is more of a parallelogram with the sides slightly skewed to follow setback lines from neighboring properties. The original plan called for a doughnut hole through the center of the cube with living and dining on one side and bedrooms on the other. It was a bold idea designed to break the tyranny of the generic modern box, but as the plan evolved, the hole morphed into a glassed-in breezeway to allow for more practical circulation patterns among interior spaces.

The front facade was broken into three unequal volumes that read from left to right as opaque, transparent, opaque. They also read as big, small, and medium. The largest volume, to the east, is clad in horizontal cedar siding with only two slitlike windows breaking the surface. This volume contains living, dining, and kitchen with a master bedroom suite above. The central foyer section is glassed in on both north and south sides and is more of an anti-volume, retaining a vestige of the original void. It encloses a signature Barnes Coy staircase with a single steel stringer, floating teak treads, and stainless steel handrail. With a skylight at the top and glass on both sides, this vertical circulation core also functions as a light well, illuminating almost every room in the house. A prefabricated, industrial-type staircase hovers over the entryway like an architectural appendage and leads up to the roof-deck and distant views across the sound.

WALL

Fontini House

It was a rough, windswept site, wedged between a high, sandy ridge and a road that winds through a forest of pitch pine and scrub oak. The house was built near the point where Long Island's South Fork becomes a narrow isthmus, only a mile in width, between Napeague Harbor on one side and the Atlantic on the other. The most desirable views were to the south, looking over a sandy landscape that crosses the Montauk Highway and continues down to the ocean, less than a mile from the house.

"We had the surveyor put a stake at the highest point of the property and worked from there," said Coy. The main floor was built about four feet above that point and the top of the hill had to be excavated to create the lower floors. The architects knew from the start that they wanted the roadside to be opaque and the ocean side to be as transparent as possible. They started with the idea of a wall running east to west and using it to separate public from private spaces. There would be three levels on the north side and two levels on the south, including a double-story volume for living and dining.

A thirty-two-foot-high wall of Alabama limestone anchors the house to its two-acre perch. The wall acts as a structural grounding, an organizing principle, that features alternating bands of rugged rock face (six inches wide) and honed face (eighteen inches wide) to create a textured rhythm that not only defines the exterior but carries the rest of the house as an archaic element, suggestive of an ancient ruin or temple wall, while counterbalancing and enhancing the modernist elements of the design. "We wanted to maintain the power of that three-foot-thick stone mass throughout the house," said Coy.

The massive wall is what you notice first upon arrival and is what you remember after you've departed. It also serves to block the noise of traffic passing on the nearby road, but most of all, the wall serves as a foil for the changing light: absorbing the moody grays of an overcast morning in October or reflecting the direct rays of a mid-August sun.

The broad steps of the adjacent stone staircase appear to grow directly out of the rustic wall as they lead up to the main entrance and into an all-glass foyer furnished solely with a pimento-red side table. "We needed some kind of a mediator between inside and outside," said Coy. This crystalline portico is a freestanding entity that further emphasizes the modern-versus-archaic themes that define the interior. (One observer compared the house to a spaceship crashing into the ruins of an Irish monastery.) A window-cum-skylight breaks the parapet line at the top of the wall to reveal structure and thickness and to enhance the sense of scale.

opposite page: A thirty-two-foot-high wall of Alabama limestone runs east to west and penetrates the outer membrane of house.

pages 168–169: A cantilevered deck protrudes from the limestone wall and reaches toward ocean views.

pages 170–171: The cedar-clad volume features eighteen-foot-high openings on each side for breezes and views.

page 172: Stairwell to the second floor.

page 173: A limestone wall creates a textured rhythm that carries through the interior as a key organizing principle.

Once inside, the wall continues in a westward direction but becomes smoother in places, less rugged, more domesticated, as it establishes an internal division between private and public spaces and turns into the central chimney mass with a long, horizontal opening for the fireplace. The sheer physicality of the wall is reaffirmed, and one becomes aware of its gravitational pull when passing from the living-dining area into the kitchen, or to the main staircase that leads up to the bedroom level and continues farther aloft to a roof-deck with views of Gardiners Bay and the ocean.

There are squares within squares, and circles inscribing other circles. A supersize box made from horizontal cedar siding intersects with the limestone wall and projects southward with a cantilevered deck. This cubic volume is penetrated by a circular skylight and eighteen-foot-high openings on either side to take advantage of the prevailing southwest breezes. The circular void above is mirrored by a larger circle in the form of an exterior balcony off the master bedroom and also supports a small office that hangs over the main living-dining area. This part of the house pushes even farther out from the body of the house toward ocean views within a twenty-foot-high glass cube that repeats the shape of the crystal foyer—but on a larger scale.

above: A circular exterior skylight echoes the curving deck off the mezzanine and master bedroom.

opposite page: The cantilevered deck and swimming pool extend to the south of the house.

pages 176–177: Circular exterior skylight.

page 178: (Left) The circular exterior skylight. (Right) Cutting and layering with light.

page 179: The interior walls feature alternating bands of rugged versus polished surfaces.

pages 180–181: The limestone staircase against the massive wall defines a ceremonial entry sequence and introduces an archaic element to a modernist plan.

See plans of the Fontini House on page 284.

TRUE NORTH

Nathanson House

The 7,000-square-foot house was built on Dune Road, just to the west of the Ponquogue Bridge, not far from the iconic Pearlroth House by Andrew Geller. From the start, it was clearly going to be a house with two sides, two personalities. Elyse Nathanson wanted a simple beach house that evoked the seaside memories of her youth, whereas her husband wanted something bigger, more ambitious, what he called an "ambidextrous house," that would face both Shinnecock Bay to the north and the Atlantic Ocean to the south. (The property is in a highly vulnerable flood zone threatened by hurricane surge.)

Barnes Coy came up with an ingenious bipolar structure that addressed both bodies of water while solving the problems of the narrow, one-acre lot that was further constricted by environmental restrictions on all sides, including a 17-foot setback to the east and a 125-foot setback from the primary dune.

At first, the clients were uneasy about building a modernist house. They preferred a more conventional dwelling, but the architects explained how a neo-traditional house would be less flexible and wouldn't be able to have the kind of expansive views and openness that a modern house could offer.

Although the clients eventually agreed, they remained adamant about not wanting a flat roof. So the architects came up with a variation of Marcel Breuer's "binuclear" houses of the 1950s. The roof dips down in the middle and flares upward at either end, like the wings of a butterfly, hence the name, "butterfly roof." It not only breaks the predictability of a conventional pitched roof but gives the house a more buoyant presence that verges on hovering. The roof planes jut out at either end with deeply cantilevered, twelve-foot overhangs to further emphasize the floating, winglike metaphor.

The entry side of the house features a grid of teak beams rising off a plinth of roughly finished fieldstone. While the hefty beams and stone foundation physically anchor the house to its shifting, sandy site, the Barnes Coy design was conceptually anchored by a slender strip of stainless steel, embedded in the ground floor as an indicator of true north. "I wanted to ground the house to its location," said Coy, who was inspired by the prime meridian line at the Royal Observatory in Greenwich, England. "There's a basic truth to it." The rest of the house grew around this north-south alignment in a bipartite fashion. Indeed, the structure appears to be cleaved down the middle, from north to south, and while integrated from within, the house expresses itself as two separate pavilions that have been fused together in a longitudinal fashion, like tectonic plates.

opposite page: A long, narrow boardwalk leads from the seven-thousand-square-foot house to the crest of the ocean dune.

pages 184–185: A wedge-shaped opening cleaves the house into two sections.

page 186: The so-called "ambidextrous house" faces the Atlantic Ocean on one side and Shinnecock Bay on the other.

page 187: Cantilevered decks hover over the swimming pool.

Wherever the two sections intersect, they create a conjunction of angular planes, converging, sometimes colliding. These chasmlike voids take on the form of staircases, skylights, trapezoidal openings, and add further to a sense of geologic fracturing. The north-south orientation is accentuated by a terrace and swimming pool that stretch along the western side of the house and lead to a narrow wooden catwalk that extends all the way over the dunes to the beach.

The western half of the house contains the master bedroom suite with a private study, terrace, and outdoor shower. The eastern half is substantially larger with two living rooms—one that looks north to the wetlands and Shinnecock Bay, the other that looks south to the ocean—and it's here that the house appears to be stretching its neck toward the million-dollar water view with its flaring roofline and wildly cantilevered decks. The kitchen-dining area is separated from the ocean-side living room by a fireplace mass made from the same gray fieldstone the architects used for the foundation plinth. The lower level has space for several guest bedrooms, as well as a children's recreation area and a fitness room for the parents.

above: Detail of the exterior staircase.

opposite page: The exterior staircase leads down to the pool terrace.

pages 190–191: The cantilevered living room reaches over the pool terrace south toward the ocean beach.

See plans of the Nathanson House on page 284.

TRANSLUCENCE

Rye House

While a summer dream house in the Hamptons might be a pure expression of aspiration, status, and expectation, a year-round residence calls for a more discrete set of spatial hierarchies. Rye, New York, is a busy commuter town, only thirty miles from Wall Street, and the waterfront site presented a more buttoned-down suburban context. Houses are closer together, and the landscape is more subdued than the wild ocean dunes of Long Island. Barnes Coy's plan was a response to a series of challenging conditions, including the bulging shape of the waterfront lot and a series of environmental restrictions that made for a tightly constricted building envelope. The site points eastward across the waters of Long Island Sound, a vista that is only interrupted here and there by small islands—Forbes Rocks, Forlies Rocks—that rise as craggy, uninhabited protuberances.

The architects' brief was to maximize water views while blocking out neighboring houses. Preliminary studies show the intersection of two fully transparent volumes raised on slender, sticklike columns, and anchored by a masonry chimney at the center. This early scheme was open and light and called for the barest skeletal structure. Due to the client's desire to have greater privacy and less direct sunlight, some of the airy, skeletal quality of the initial studies was lost in the final proposal. Instead, the sense of lightness and transparency was filtered inward and upward with intersecting levels and layers that peel away like the translucent skins of an onion, open and exposed in some places, veiled in others.

The entry facade is broken into two autonomous elements: one transparent, the other largely opaque. The upper level is wrapped in horizontal teak siding and angles outward to create an overhang for shade and to interrupt the geometric severity of the proverbial glass box. A sweeping lateral movement is created by the slats of a sixty-foot-long brise-soleil—something like hyperextended Venetian blinds—that stretches to the south end of the house and shields the upstairs gallery from direct sunlight.

L-shaped steps made from blocks of bluestone lead from the forecourt through a slablike doorway made from laminated teak. The sensually minimal foyer sets the tone for the rest of the interior. A walnut screen blocks out a neighbor to the north, and a wall of acid-etched marble is spotlighted by a configuration of semispheric sconces. The dramatically cantilevered staircase ascends a two-story void that lies between the curtain wall on one side and the living room on the other. "We wanted to reveal the internal organs of the house and create a correspondence between the first and second levels," explained Coy. Illuminated from above by a long, narrow

opposite page: The master bedroom suite hangs above a loggia supported by a single steel column.

pages 194–195: The upper level of the entry façade projects above a glass curtain wall. A sixty-foot-long brise soleil is made from horizontal slats of teak and shields the upstairs gallery from sunlight.

pages 196–198: The living room floats between transparent membranes to the east and west.

See plans of the Rye House on page 285.

skylight, this wedgelike space emphasizes both the vertical and horizontal dimensions of the plan.

The engineering—teak treads, steel stringer, all-glass safety railings—is fully showcased through the curtain wall and is one of the first things you notice when approaching the property. Together, the brise-soleil, curtain wall, and see-through railings create a multilayered set of crystalline membranes, as if the front facade had been delaminated. From there, the open plan unfolds in several directions.

The main living and dining area floats between two transparencies to the east and west. Interior furnishings (Julia Roth Design) have simple, modern forms and a muted palette to complement the architecture: Danish modern chairs, and a slab of dark walnut for the dining table that is lit from above by a grid of twinkling lights. Most of the built-in millwork was custom-made by cabinetmaker Ian Ingersoll, including a low walnut console that conceals the television screen while dividing the living from dining areas.

Upstairs, a narrow balcony steps back from the stairwell and leads to five bedrooms, including the master suite. A smaller version of the staircase continues upward, into the open air, liberating itself from the confines of the interior as it ascends to a spacious roof-deck that has been built for outdoor living with a fireplace, built-in bar, and kitchen.

Further below, at the clients' request, Barnes Coy inserted a fully equipped gym, several guest rooms, and a recreation room that looks into the swimming pool through a wall of glass, something like a human aquarium. To allow for such a spacious basement with twelve-foot ceilings, the builders were obliged to dig down into Westchester bedrock, blasting and drilling out several tons of granite. "It was as if we'd opened a quarry," recalled Coy.

The house's L-shaped plan (what the architects refer to as a "Dog with a Bone") turns away from the looming neighbor to the south and creates a privacy barrier on the water side that shields the pool terrace area. The entry forecourt is equally protected by a one-story garage and stucco wall that runs along the same south boundary. The shorter section of the "L"—the so-called bone—breaks the plane of the all-glass facade and projects out toward the sound, while housing the master bedroom suite with a private deck that is cantilevered toward water views and supported by a single column. Directly below is an open-air loggia with gas fireplace that looks out over the terrace and zero-edge swimming pool. The eastern side of the pool is bowed out to echo yet another environmental setback, the "Moderate Wave Action" line, while the natural grade slopes down four to five feet as it nears the water's edge. To compensate for the drop in elevation, house and terrace are raised on a plinth of Westchester granite rustically stacked in two-inch strips to blend in with the rocky shoreline and seawall.

opposite page: The main staircase with teak treads and glass safety railings appears to climb all the way to the roof deck.

pages 200–201: The marble fireplace mass and teak wall define the northern end of the living room.

page 202: (Left) The front entrance light fixture by Massimo Castagna. (Right) A juxtaposition of light-reflecting materials.

page 203: Details of the teak, glass and steel staircase.

page 204: The upper-level gallery hangs over a wedge-shaped lightwell and creates a third layer of spatial organization.

page 205: Painting by Ulrike Arnold.

pages 206–207: Master bathroom.

page 208: The upper level is slightly skewed off its axis to break the severity of the proverbial modern box.

page 209: Poolside facade with the exterior shower and grill.

page 210: Details of the master bedroom balcony (above), and the staircase (below).

page 211: Detail of the chandelier (above), and the horizontal louvers of the brise-soleil (below).

pages 212–213: Exterior steps to the roof deck.

pages 214–215: The L-shaped plan with overlapping planes that reflect the shape of the waterfront lot and blocks out the neighboring house while directing views across the Long Island Sound.

SWAMP THING

Baxter/Bray House

Tidal creeks branch off from the Julienton River, twisting and turning like retinal veins. When the water drains out to Saint Catherines Sound, it leaves little footprints, so you can tell where the birds have pecked among the needlerush and sawgrass and left their marks in slimy sediment: wood storks, cormorants, herons, ibis, egrets, an entire glossary of birdsongs cross-pollinating. Furtive populations of frogs and fiddler crabs skitter across the spongy peat and root clusters and there's a reddish hue to the spiky spartina that slowly shifts to a sage gray and pale green as the day progresses, giving shape to light.

Low-country locals have a special name for the tidal sediment; they call it "pluff mud." The Harris Neck House appears to grow right out of the pluff mud itself, perched as it is on top of forty-foot-tall cypress tree trunks that were harvested from the swamp and appear to grow through the full height of the house.

The homeowners and their three children are passionate about wildlife and the unique lowland ecology of coastal Georgia. The wife grew up in Georgia; the husband is from Canada. They spend most of the year in Hong Kong but come here for their summer vacations. At the end of the day, when the tide rolls back, they walk to the end of the 180-foot-long pier and watch the baitfish move in from the bay as they're pursued by dolphins, alligators, and an occasional bull shark.

In plan, the house cranks to the north, like a swamp creature, hovering high on its thirteen legs of cypress, and following the bend of the bay, wrapping around the outer fringes of swamp to maximize views and expand a westward exposure. Toward the back, or eastern side of the house, grows an enchanted woodland of loblolly pines, cypress, gnarled oaks draped with Spanish moss, pitch pine, and southern magnolia.

The house is raised twenty feet above the floodplain, like Noah's Ark awaiting the flood, and the hull-like impression is enhanced by the fact that the exterior is clad in horizontal shiplap. The massive cypress trunks create a rustic loggia below the house with a flagstone terrace surrounded by philodendron and other tropical vegetation. A screened-in platform hangs from the ceiling and makes a perfect perch for watching sunsets. This odd, underhanging deck is reached from above by a narrow staircase, or from below by a ladder.

The sidewalls of the long, narrow wing are canted outward with sloping panes of custom-engineered glass that flood the interior with swamp-reflected light while drawing the eye out toward the salt marshes of Harris Neck River on one side, and the wetlands of a wildlife refuge on the other.

opposite page: The facade of roughly faceted Pennsylvania fieldstone anchors the south end of the house to the Georgia swamp setting.

pages 218–219: Rough blocks of fieldstone contrast with prismatic wood volumes.

page 220: The house is elevated twenty feet above the flood plain on thirteen massive cypress logs harvested from a nearby swamp.

page 221: The screened-in porch hangs from the undercroft to provide 360-degree views of marsh wilderness.

pages 222–223: Specially engineered windows lean out at an angle to provide views of the surrounding terrain; cypress columns penetrate the interior space.

page 224: Partitions made from Alaskan yellow cedar divide public and private spaces.

page 225: Yellow pine floors, cedar walls, and cypress columns absorb the swamp-reflected light.

page 226: Wood box windows of the kitchen and dining rooms are set in blocks of fieldstone.

page 227: The structure of the main staircase reveals itself through a glass casing.

pages 228–229: Artfully rendered details of the loggia, screen door, and inner staircases.

pages 230–231: The flood-proof house set in the sprawling wetlands of the Harris Neck National Wildlife Refuge.

opposite page: The table is set for Sunday lunch overlooking Blackbeard Creek and the surrounding swamp.

above: A cedar walkway leads to a viewing platform and tea house that overlook the salt marshes.

pages 234–235: Swamp Thing lit up at night.

See plans of the Baxter/Bray House on page 285.

Interior spaces combine the minimal lines of a modernist pavilion with the Zen simplicity of a Japanese teahouse. A steel-framed staircase straddles the masonry mass at the south end and leads to a roof-deck. The overhead skylight creates the effect of a luminous waterfall cascading down the rugged stone wall. Objects and people take on a spectral, drifting quality in the moisture-laden light that pours in from all sides. The cypress tree trunks thrust all the way through the main living space and quite literally bring the wilderness inside. Floors are made from southern yellow pine, while Alaskan yellow cedar panels were shaped to fit the diagonally sloping outer walls and provide a shiplike division of space. The different wood surfaces complement one another and give the architecture a quiet, almost meditative presence. Even some of the door handles have been fashioned from gnarled pieces of local cypress.

The north end has bedrooms for the children and a master bedroom suite that's tucked into the narrow "prow" of the house with three-sided views and a bathroom that enjoys views of Blackbeard Creek through a wall of floor-to-ceiling glass. The opposite end of the house is anchored to the flood-prone site by a three-story blockhouse of gray Pennsylvania fieldstone and contains the main entryway, staircase, guest bedroom suite, and kitchen. Rough blocks of stone jut out randomly from the southern section, creating short ledges so as to break up the monotony of the surface and create a sense of rustication and ruin. Indeed, the entire house could be seen as a kind of ruin in reverse.

INFINITY

Koch House II

A narrow road leads south from Manzanillo across the hilly, lizard-shaped peninsula of Papagayo, and past the Santa Rosa National Park, a nature sanctuary with more than 120,000 acres of unspoiled wilderness. The house itself is called "Cielo Mar" after the sky and sea. Its borders seem edgeless, almost infinite, more like a series of articulated events than a single architectural statement. Internal spaces are peripheral and much less hierarchical than a conventional home, almost as if the architects had taken the elements of a generic vacation house, pulled them apart, and stretched them into a curving mantle.

As always, the design began with the topography of the surrounding hills, which are thick with vegetation: strangler figs, banyans, papaya, bamboo, yucca, and walking palms, growing right up to the edge of the site. Small spider monkeys cling to the overhanging trees. At night you can hear the mantled howlers screaming from the depths of the jungle, like abandoned souls.

On their first day of discovery, Barnes and Coy noticed how all the neighboring houses were perched high along the top of the cliff, which, to the architects, seemed predictable, almost suburban. "We wanted something that responded to the immediate environment," said Coy, who sat with Barnes watching the sunset and came up with the idea of having a low, one-story profile above the ridge while making the rest of the house "dribble down" the side of the cliff with additional levels. It came to the architects in a flash of inspiration, a way to create privacy from the street and allow for more square footage.

Barnes Coy's final design would turn everyday living into an acrobatic balance among sea, sky, and landscape. The architecture is interactive and performative. The roof slides skyward in a double-compound curve that is structurally buttressed by five steel columns and supports an array of solar panels, which supply more than 50 percent of the house's energy needs, including air-conditioning. The crescent shape of the overall plan mirrors, almost exactly, the curve of the cliff and Playa Prieta, a sandy beach that lies directly below the property. The curve breaks up the 11,500-square-foot mass of the house and allows every room a water view. The most prominent feature is a long linear platform that penetrates the house's outer curve through a central portal and continues to project out toward the Pacific Ocean like a bridge to nowhere—an elegant engineering folly with the sole purpose of watching sunsets. Stainless steel tension cables support the ninety-foot-long walkway that uses the same engineering principles as a cable-stayed

opposite page: A stone wall with a six-foot-square opening defines the south end of the pool deck.

pages 238–239: An 11,500-square-foot house steps down from the crest of the hill in three terraced levels; the plan mirrors the curving shape of cliff.

suspension bridge. The architects aimed it due west, directly toward the setting sun, and it became the central trope for the entire project. (At this latitude, the sun goes down in more or less the same place every evening.) Two inclined struts lean out on either side and support the weight of the catwalk with thick cables attached to turnbuckles.

Indeed, it feels as if the entire house were held in place by a kind of trapezelike tension. There's a humming vibration whenever the wind blows, and the elongated catwalk and floating staircases move up and down when you walk on them. Large triangular canopies, stitched like genoa jibs, can be raised or adjusted for shade by pulling nylon halyards through self-tailing Harken winches. During earthquakes, everything in the house buckles quite effortlessly in concert with the trembling earth.

Because of such severe seismic activity, the house had to be anchored to its precipitous site with several terraced foundation levels and deeply embedded retaining walls. The sloping earth and volcanic rock were fully encased in concrete while steel-reinforced "dead-man" beams were buried fifty feet into the ground so that the house wouldn't slide down the steep hillside. (A recent 7.6 earthquake shook the house quite severely but caused no significant damage.)

From the street, the house makes a surprisingly low-key profile—modern but restrained—with nothing to indicate the gymnastics that lie on the other side of the white stucco facade. Its convex geometry is emphasized by tiers of textured grass that echo the curve of the front wall. Orange I-beams support an entry canopy and boardwalk that lead through the five-foot-wide entry portal. As soon as you pass through this outer membrane, everything changes, and the architecture erupts. A narrow, upward-rising gallery leads to family bedrooms and a study. Below that lies the master bedroom suite that looks out onto a sunken Zen garden that has been landscaped with black bamboo, smooth river stones, and a single, red-leafed Malinche tree.

A fully enclosed living and dining area ("salon") is tucked into the northern end of the house's sweeping arc. Although it's hardly ever used during dry winter months (November to March), during the rainy season (April to October), it becomes the central space for dining and family gathering. Floor-to-ceiling glass wraps around the front and the back wall bulges out to make way for a landmark Laurel Negro tree that needed to be preserved. The back wall is painted with a bright abstract mural by Austrian artist Andrea Bischof that effectively breaks the monotony of this blank, windowless wall.

Although the architects wanted to enclose the kitchen with a two-story wall of Corten steel, they weren't able to source the material in Costa Rica. Instead they used a rust-tinted ceramic panel that wraps around the corner to become a backdrop for the daringly cantilevered staircase that leads down to a lower level with guest rooms, a gym, and a family theater.

opposite page: An inclined strut supports the end of the walkway above the infinity pool.

pages 242–243: A ninety-foot-long "sun bridge" penetrates the crescent-shaped house in line with the setting sun.

pages 244–245: The cantilevered deck projects over the infinity pool toward Pacific Ocean views.

page 246: A stone tub in the master bathroom.

page 247: Rust-colored ceramic panels enclose the blocklike volume of the kitchen.

pages 248–249: Details of interactive architecture are held together with trapezelike tension and nautical rigging.

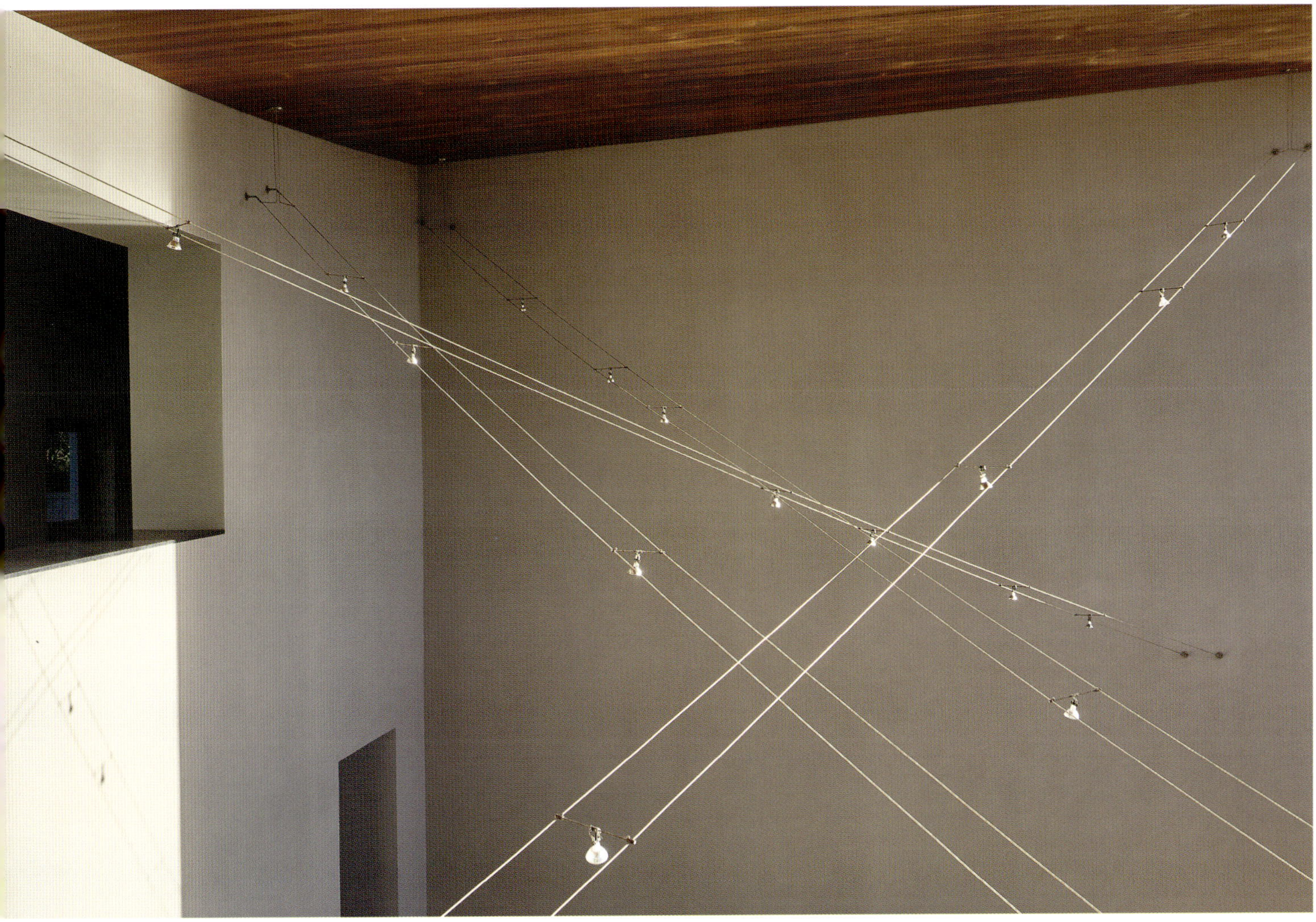

pages 250–251: The equatorial sun casts diagonal shadows through openings in the cantilevered staircase.

pages 252–253: The "sun bridge" and sails penetrate the crescent-shaped house like an arrow and bow.

opposite page: View from the entry colonnade to the end of sun the deck.

above: Sunset and cocktails on the bridge.

pages 256–257: A curving stucco facade was designed to create a low-scale presence on the street-side of the property.

See plans of the Koch House II: on page 286.

While the main deck serves as the house's central stage—animated as it is with movement, torque, and tensility—there are also quiet, less central areas where one can sit and contemplate the wilder edges of nature. The eighty-five-foot-long lap pool defines the western boundary as it mirrors the sky and carries one's eye past the edge of the deck, above the steep incline and out toward the Gulf of Papagayo. At night, giant fruit bats swoop back and forth across the pool hunting for insects. A six-foot-square opening at the far end of the deck makes an ideal perch for reading or watching turkey vultures gliding overhead, and every evening, at about 6:30 p.m., the homeowners and their guests walk to the end of the elevated bridge, drink cocktails, and grade the quality of the sunset, from one to ten.

GH DESERT

Owen House

Despite the manicured lawns and infinity pools of this gated community, there's still a sense of wilderness in the patchy brown foothills of the Santa Rosa Mountains. Just beyond the chain-link fencing are jackrabbits and bobcats, coyotes and mountain lions prowling. Early in the morning, bighorn sheep wander down from the higher ridges, coming right up to the property lines, staking out their territory. The Owen House reads, in part, as a modern desert temple, a twenty-first-century version of the Parthenon, commanding its high plateau, while paying homage to the arid hills that rise in the background. It's only a few miles from the San Andreas Fault, and the terrain is unstable, prone to earthquakes and mudslides, a fractured stratum of quartzite, clay, and fine-grained silt from seasonal runoffs, barely held in place by hardy native plants like brittlebush with its yellow bloom and ocotillo, yucca, and cholla cactus.

As one moves up the hillside from the lower vantage of Skyline Drive, perspective unfolds and the concrete forms appear to stretch out even further across the moraine, creating the illusion of greater length and complexity. The high desert light creates the sharpest of edges. Shadows are deep, verging on black. The flaring white forms stand out from the surrounding landscape, cutting cleanly across the sky and wildly rolling contours of earth.

The clients—in-laws of Chris Coy with two grown children and five grandchildren—wanted to downsize from a 7,600-square-foot house in La Quinta.

"Rob and I walked the property extensively and liked the fact that the building envelope was on a long axis, north to south," said Coy. This gave the architects a starting point and from there an overarching concept emerged, almost on a whim.

After studying a topographic survey, Barnes sat down and drew a line rising toward the north end of the plateau. Then, with hardly a thought, Coy picked up a pencil and drew a diagonal line pointing in the opposite direction. "It was the first sketch we did," recalled Coy, and this became the core idea. The scissorlike composition would lead the eye to the north and south, while the opposing, finlike extremities would echo the shape of two nearby mountains. The rest of the plan followed naturally from there, and what started out to be a modest 3,000-square-foot structure, grew to more than 5,000 square feet.

Resisting the urge to mimic local mid-century tendencies—as in the work of Albert Frey, John Lautner, William Krisel, and other Palm Springs modernists—Barnes Coy drew inspiration from a more international school of modernism, one that was derived from the

opposite page: Cast concrete fin at the southern end absorbs the desert light.

pages 260–261: Templelike proportions with sloping, interpenetrating forms that point in opposite directions, while echoing the shape of the nearby foothills.

strident Italian Rationalism of Giuseppe Terragni, Gruppo 7, and the Futurism of Antonio Sant'Elia. An opaque wedge of concrete intersects with the sloping colonnade that gives the house its distinctive profile. In fact, the colonnade was conceived as a baffle to provide privacy from the neighbors to the east while also blocking the harsh desert sun. The City of Rancho Mirage allows a maximum height of only eighteen feet above grade for residential structures, so this was one way to create the illusion of greater height. "The mountains are so huge in scale that we had to create a scale-denying strategy," said Coy.

In fact, the design is surprisingly simple. Two interpenetrating wedges are penetrated by a third, more cubic volume. Gill-like openings are sixteen feet high but compress in size as they advance toward the south, diminishing to twelve feet while coming closer together, incrementally, from thirty-nine inches at the widest, to fifteen inches on the narrow end. It's a visual trope, a kind of forced perspective, but the spacing and repetition of forms create a monumental sense of expectation. "The house is just over 5,000 square feet but we wanted to create more of a presence," said Coy. "Staggering the distance between the piers made the house seem three times as big."

In morning light, the piers cast diagonal shadows across the terrace and living room, making for a moody, film-noir effect. The colonnade marks the hours of the day like a linear sundial, measuring the arc of the sun's track as it moves across the sky. Interior spaces on the upper level project northward to views of the Coachella Valley through twenty-foot-wide panels of glass that can be slid open on steel tracks so that interior spaces merge with the exterior.

The trapezoidal pool reflects the eastern side of the colonnade house and extends the eye out past the subdivisions of Cathedral City, the dried-up arroyos and wind turbines of Thousand Palms, to the glide paths of commercial airliners descending into the Palm Springs airport, and even further out, to the snow-covered peaks of the San Jacinto range. "We wanted to create this view cannon, so you don't see anything else," said Coy. "It's like looking down the barrel of a howitzer."

While the east side of the living area is bordered by the colonnade, the west side is defined by a twenty-foot-long mass of acid-washed steel that contains a linear gas fireplace. "We wanted the fireplace to be volumetric and fairly massive," said Coy. As the day progresses, the graphite-hued patina of the fireplace wall changes in reflectivity and becomes a kind of grounding device to offset the floating, aerial feeling of the architecture. Interior furnishings are low and softly contoured, with muted colors, as if intentionally deferring to the drama of the exterior landscape. White walls, porcelain tile floors, and pale hemlock ceilings reflect ambient desert light while transparent Lucite vitrines hold the homeowners' collection of exotic artifacts—antique Chinese headdresses, indigenous Australian art, and metal figures from the Qing dynasty—as if they were suspended in the air.

opposite page: Gill-like openings create a colonnade that blocks the harsh desert sun while providing privacy from the neighboring houses.

pages 264–265: A box-like extrusion on the entry side contains the master bedroom and projects over a clapboard-style wall of aluminum.

page 266: Shadowplay on the entry steps.

page 267: Overview of the entry steps, gateway, and enclosed courtyard.

pages 268–269: Details of the staircases, recessed window, and overhanging roof treatment.

pages 270–271: Eleven-foot-high panels of glass are pushed open on steel tracks for uninterrupted views of the Coachella Valley.

opposite page: The indoor/outdoor living room overlooks the infinity pool and Coachella Valley.

above: A sunken courtyard with a gravel and cactus garden.

page 274: (Above) Master Bedroom. (Below) The twenty-foot-long fireplace mass is covered with panels of acid-washed steel.

page 275: (Above) The open-style kitchen reflects the elongated linearity of the general plan. (Below) Three slit-like openings bring natural light into the master bathroom.

pages 276–277: At night, the five-thousand- square-foot house becomes a beacon of light over the desert valley.

See plans of the Owen House on page 286.

The house continues to unfold to the south, but with a different geometry. The master bedroom suite takes the form of a boxlike extrusion that projects from the back of the house as a seemingly separate, autonomous volume. It faces onto a looping cul-de-sac with a narrow terrace and a sculptural brise-soleil made from horizontal baffles of black steel to block the sun. The doors of the four-car garage are clad in a kind of dark-gray aluminum clapboarding that extends across the entire breadth of the south facade like a pleated underskirt and offsets the smooth stucco surfaces of the upper level.

A zigzagging staircase leads through a discretely concealed gateway that pivots open with the push of a button, and into a sunken oasis with cacti, banana trees, palo verde trees, and other lush plantings. At the very center of the sunken courtyard, a rainlike veil of water splashes down into a concrete cistern. A series of cavelike guest rooms are positioned around the periphery of the courtyard.

PLANS

UPPER/MAIN

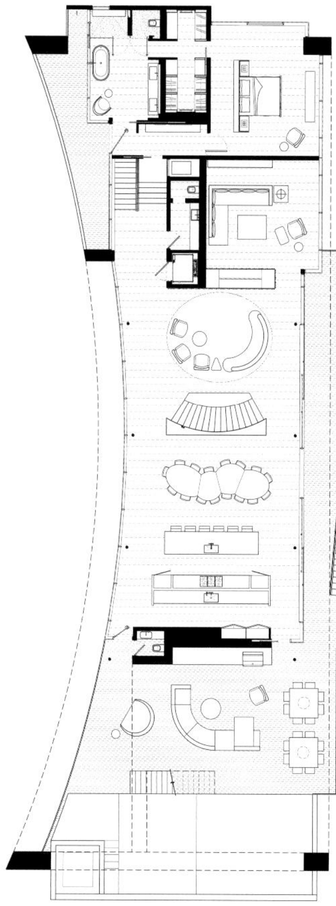

MIDDLE

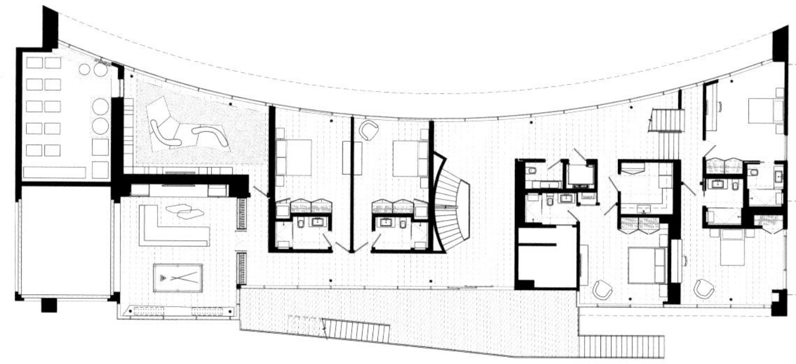

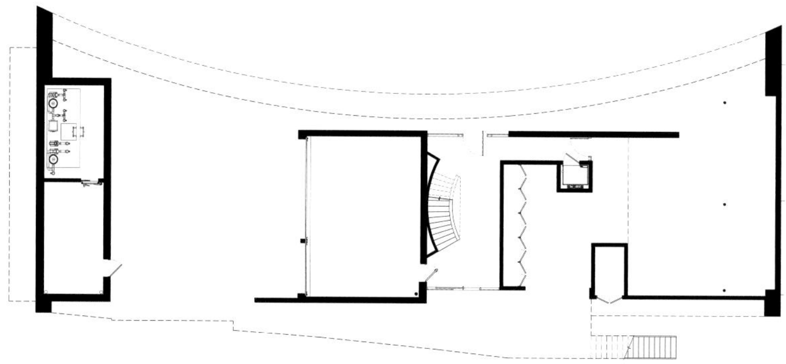

LOWER

page 26 - OCEANFRONT HOUSE

MAIN

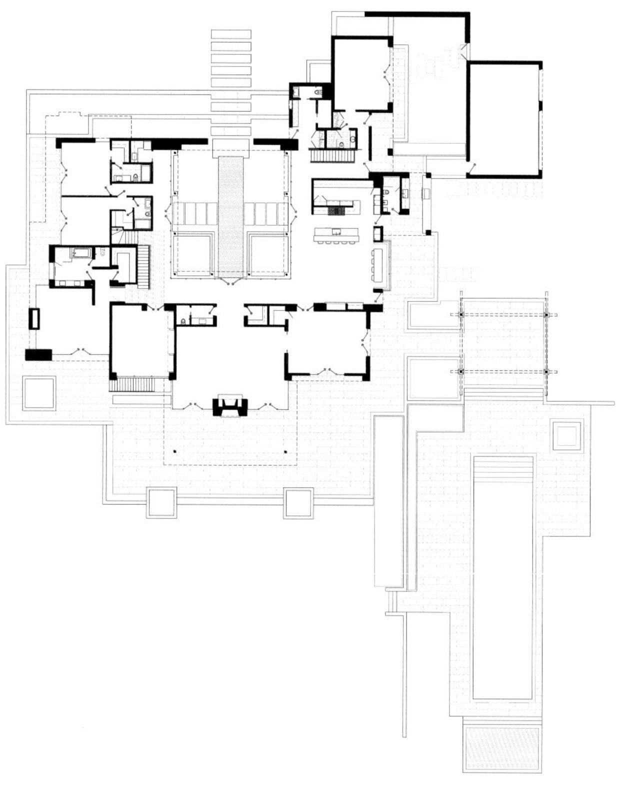

UPPER

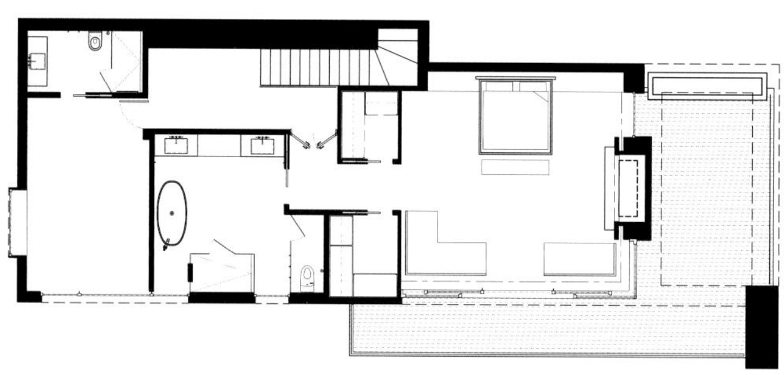

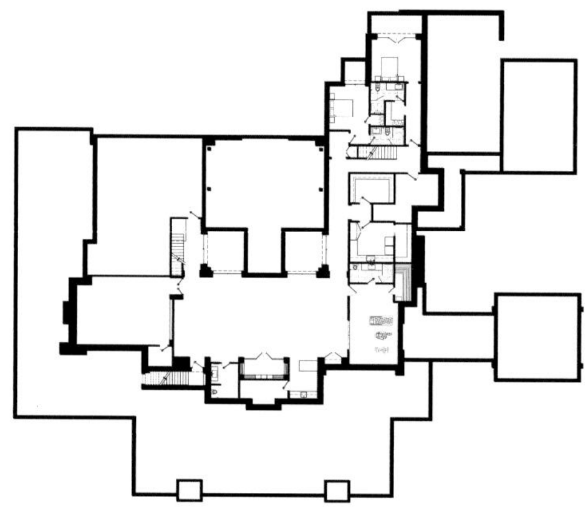

LOWER

page 50 - MEADOW HOUSE

MAIN

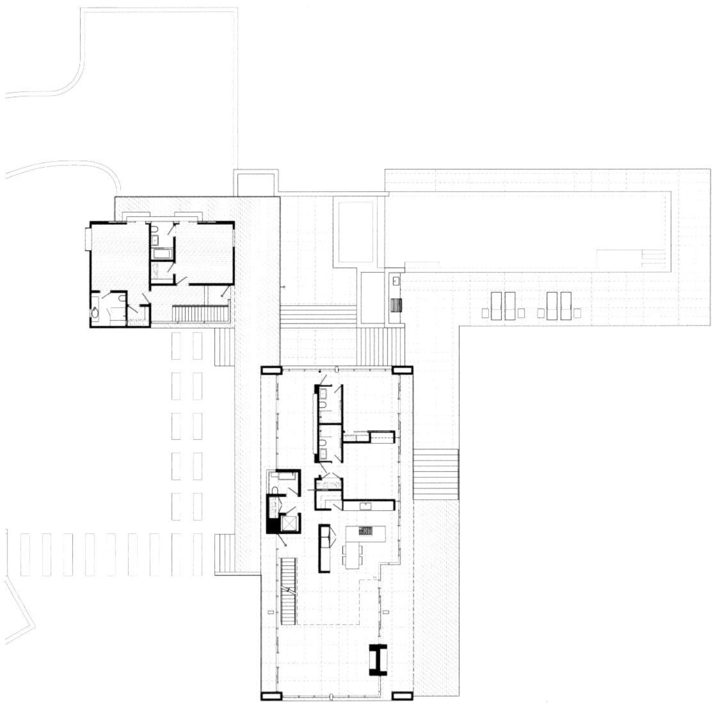

UPPER

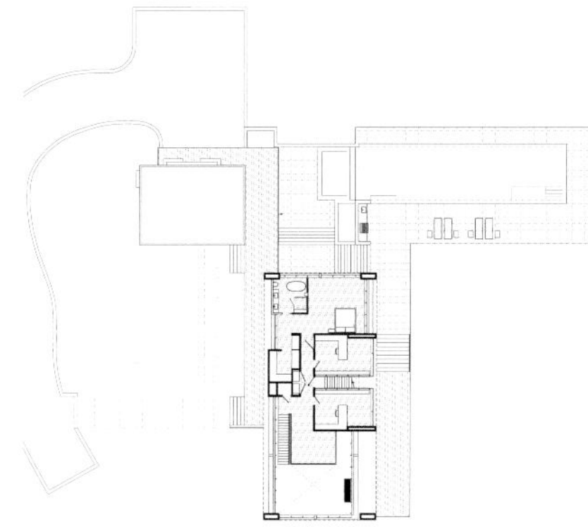

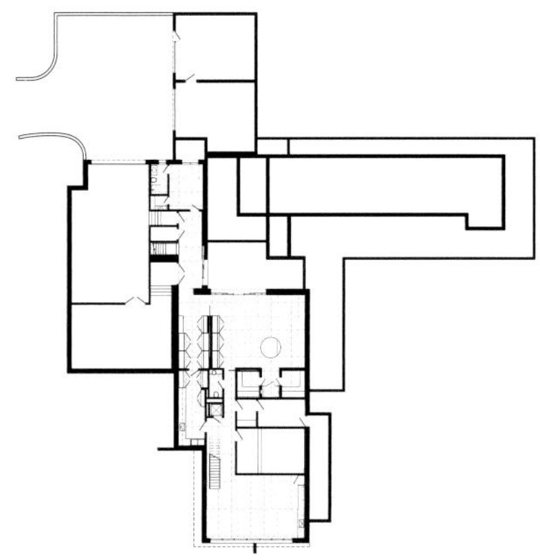

LOWER

page 72 - KOCH HOUSE I

MAIN

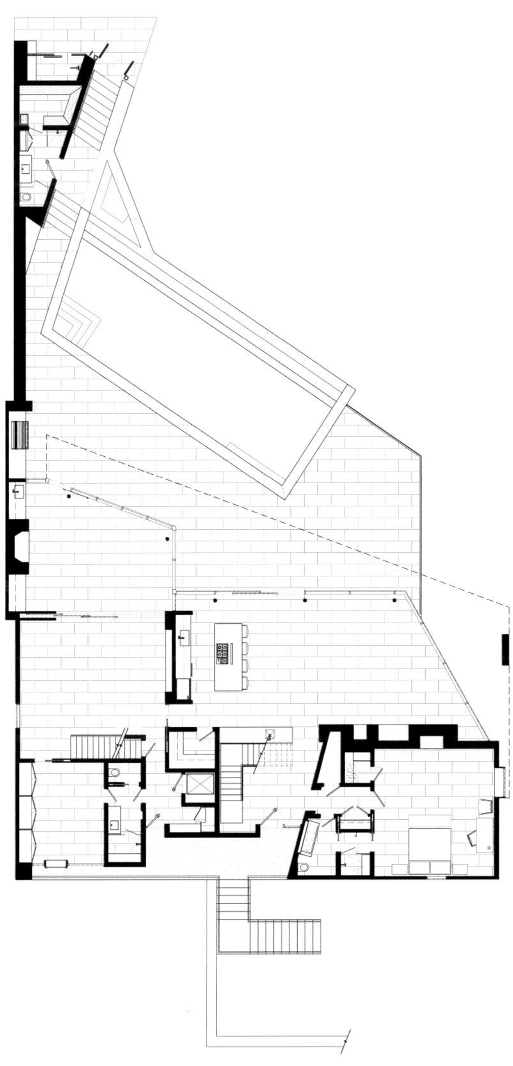

UPPER

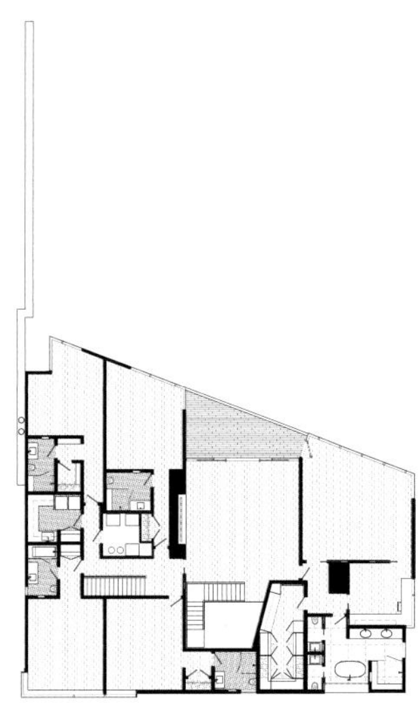

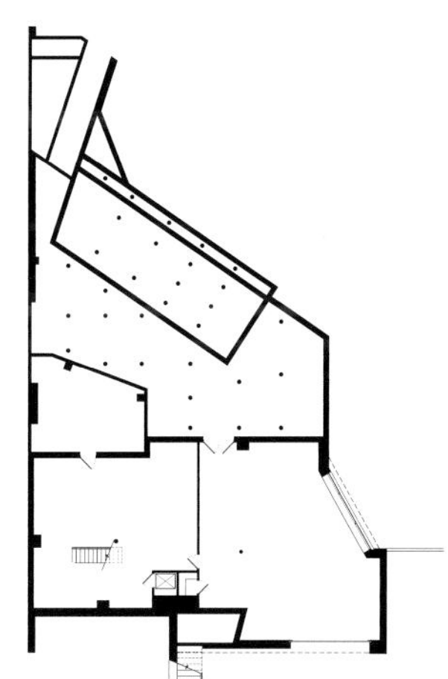

LOWER

page 88 - BAYFRONT HOUSE

MAIN

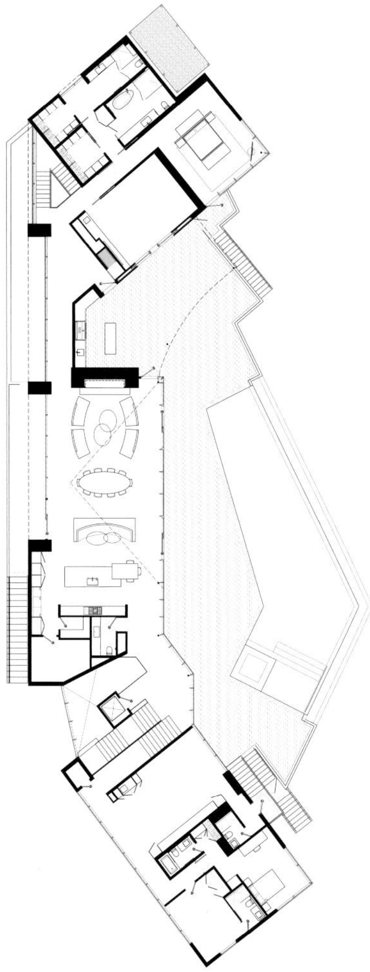

UPPER

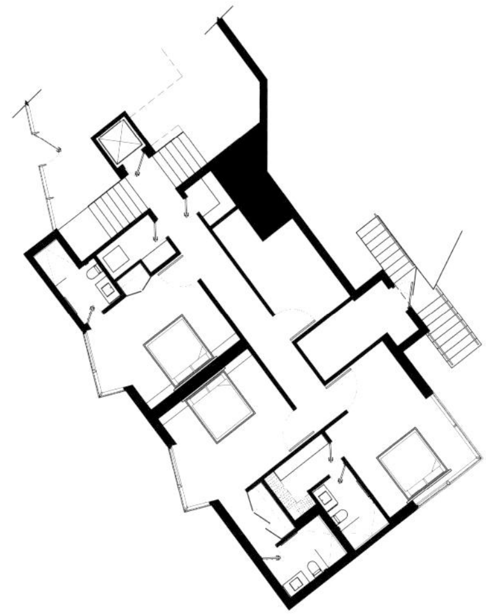

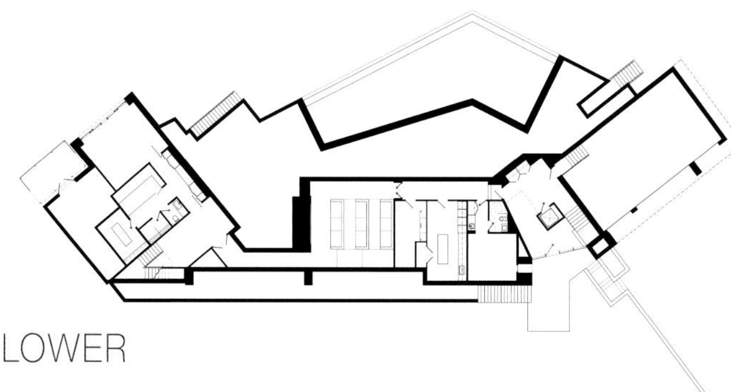

LOWER

page 102 - SUSSER HOUSE

UPPER/MAIN

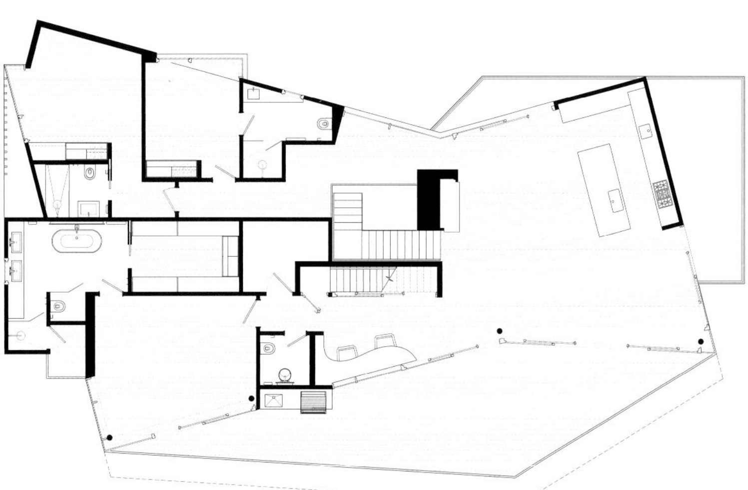

LOWER

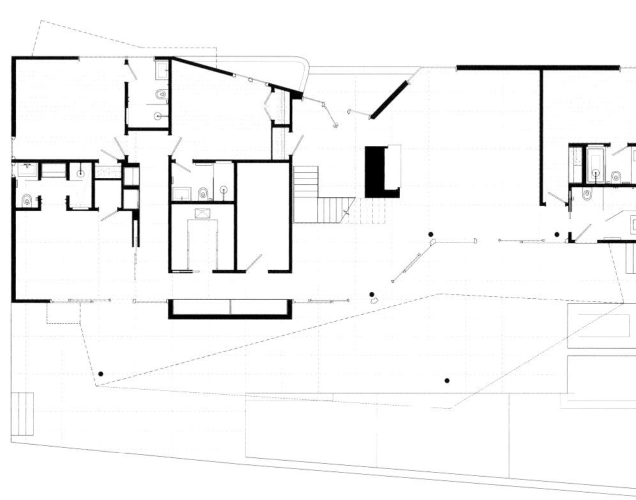

page 124 - GELFOND HOUSE

MAIN

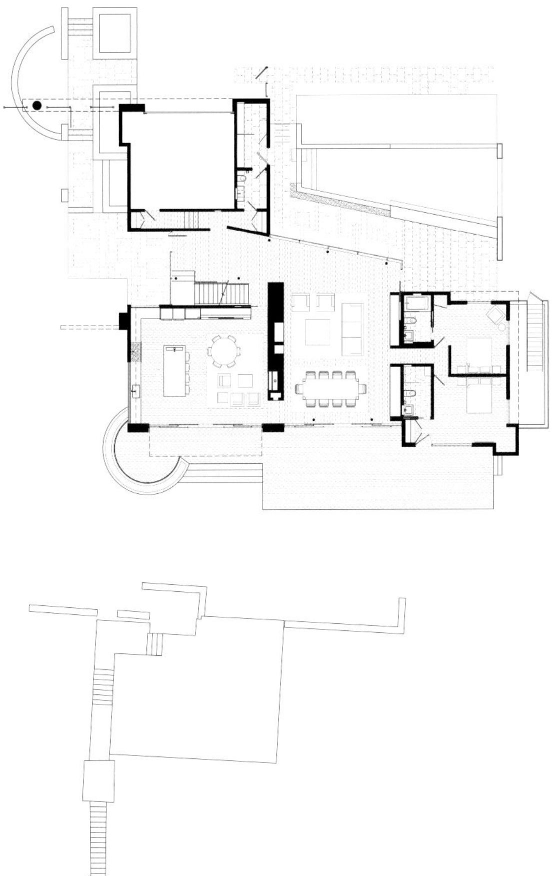

UPPER

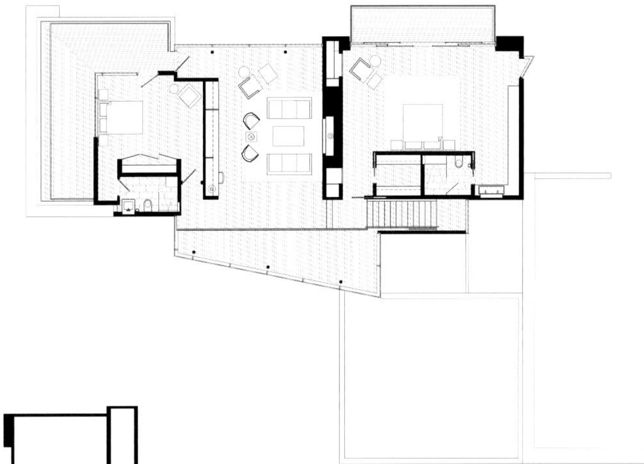

LOWER

page 134 - BECKENSTEIN/O'ROURKE HOUSE

MAIN

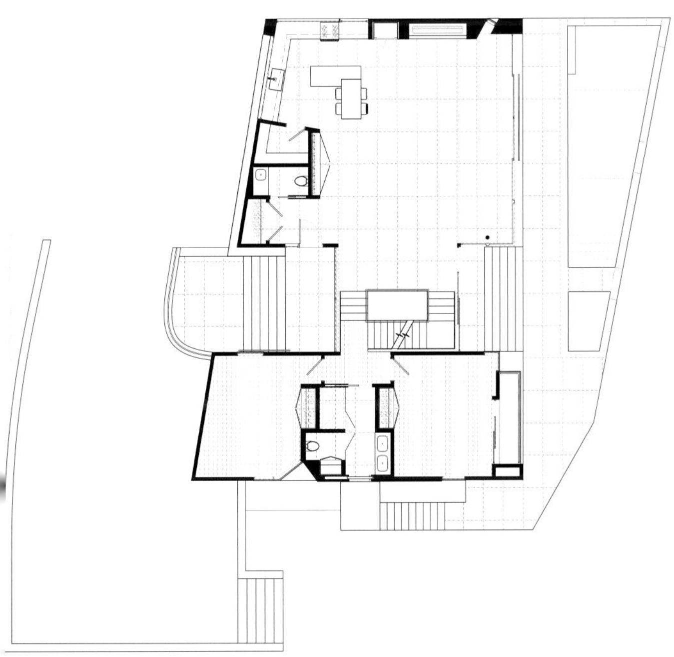

UPPER

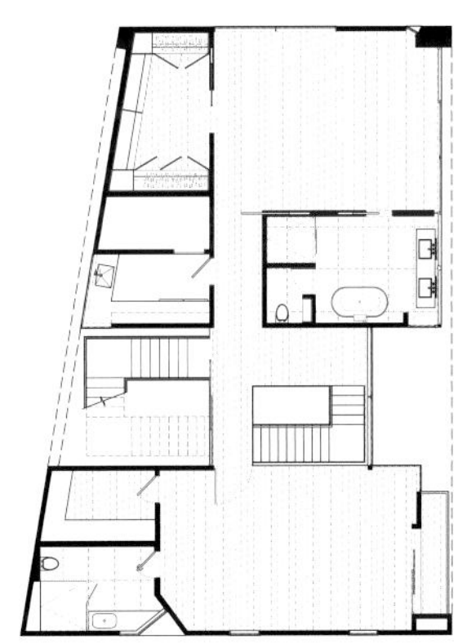

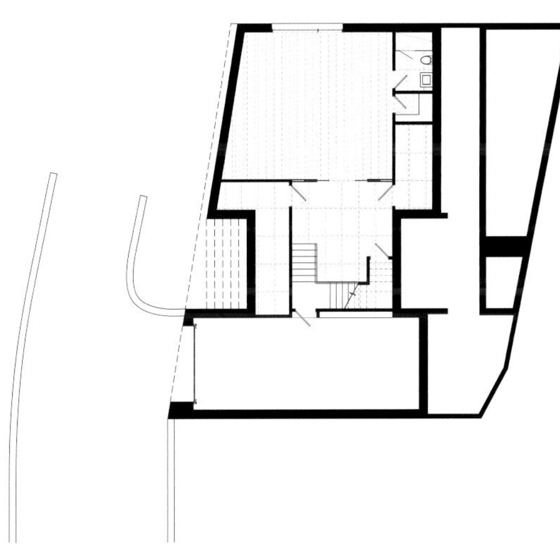

LOWER

page 154 - SEGRETE/SACK HOUSE

MAIN

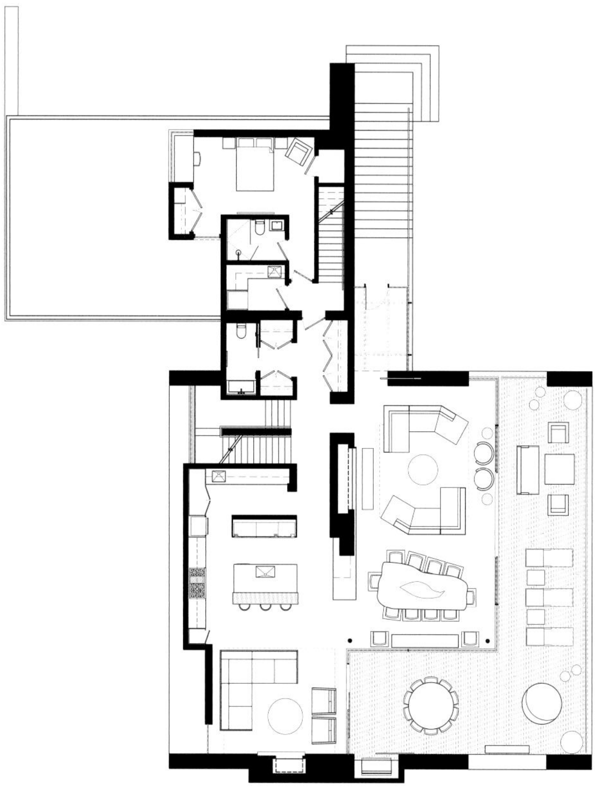

UPPER

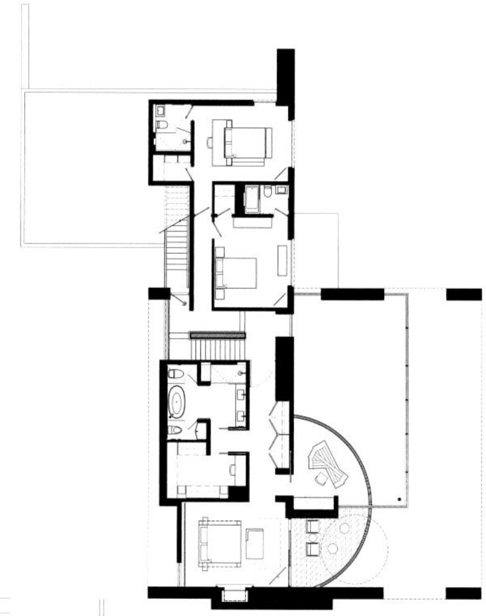

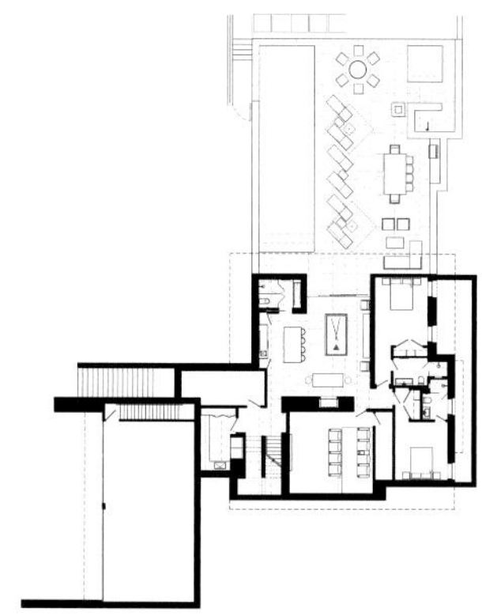

LOWER

page 166 - FONTINI HOUSE

MAIN/UPPER

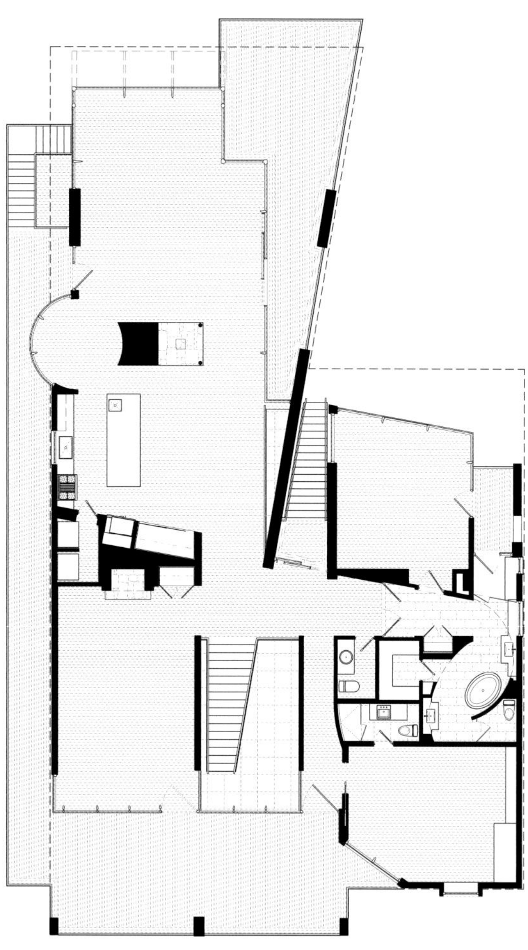

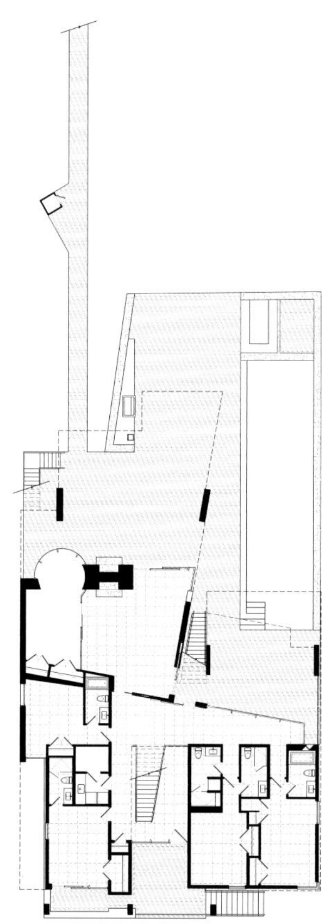

LOWER

page 182 - NATHANSON HOUSE

MAIN

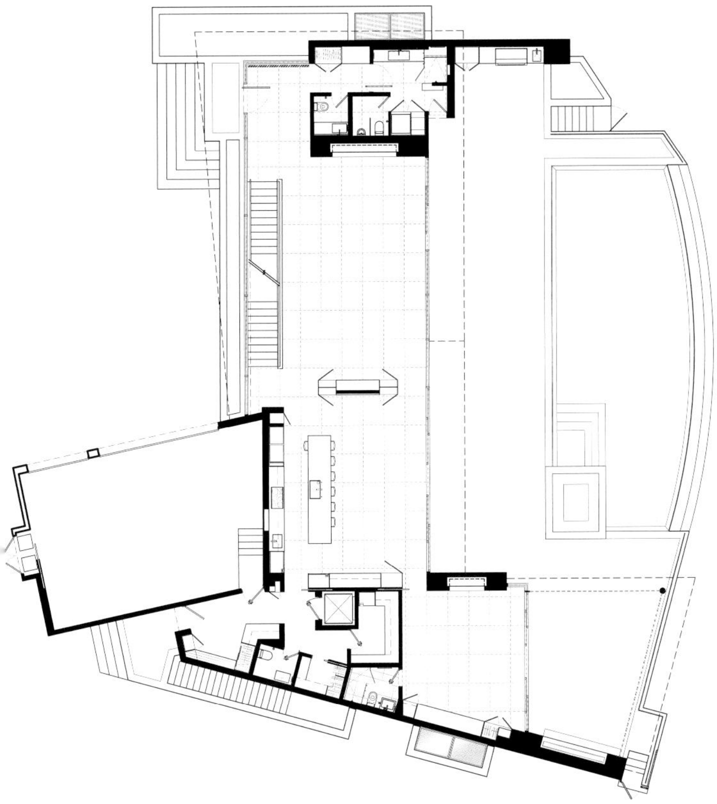

UPPER

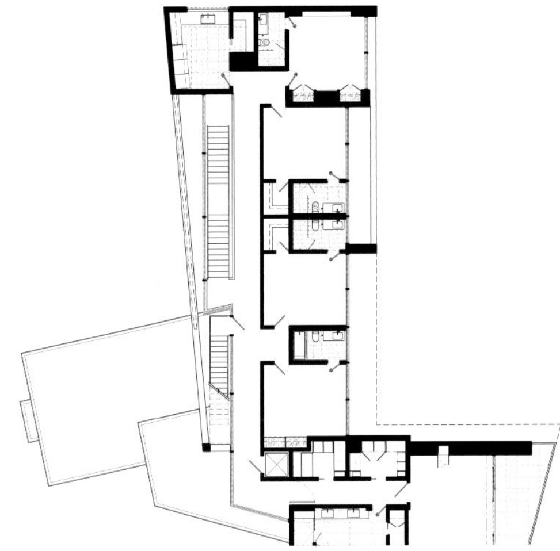

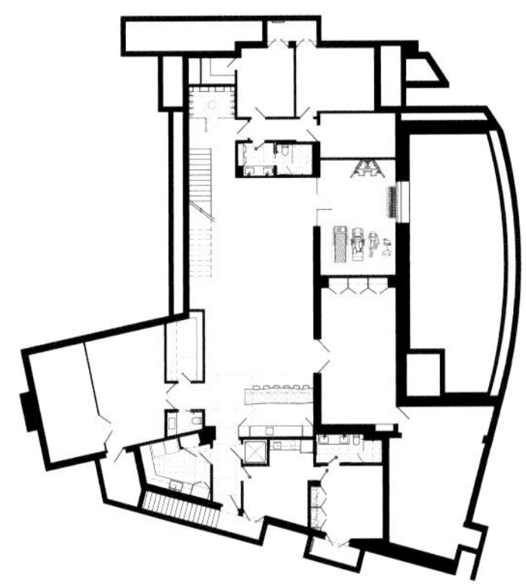

LOWER

page 192 - RYE HOUSE

MAIN

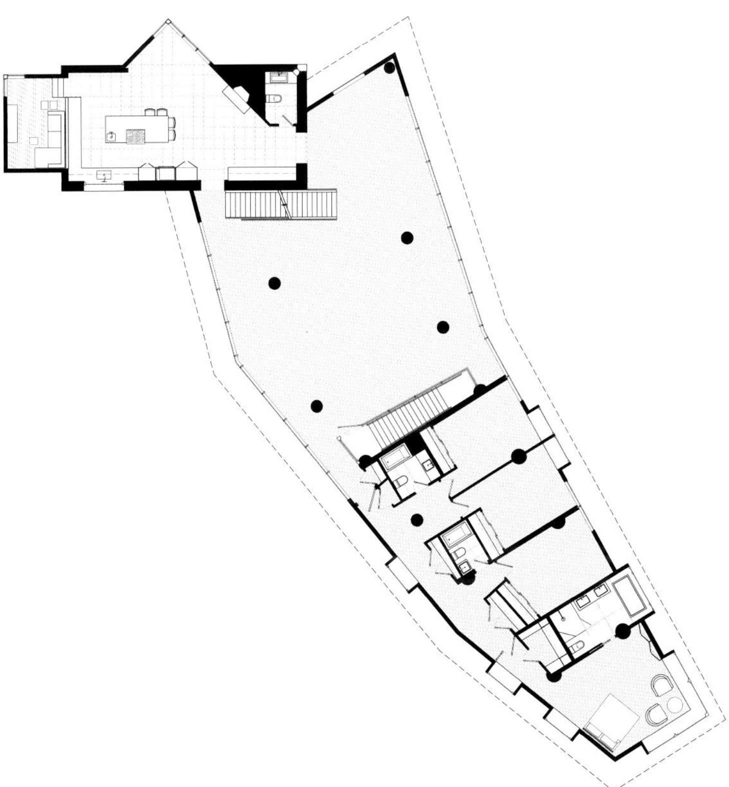

UPPER

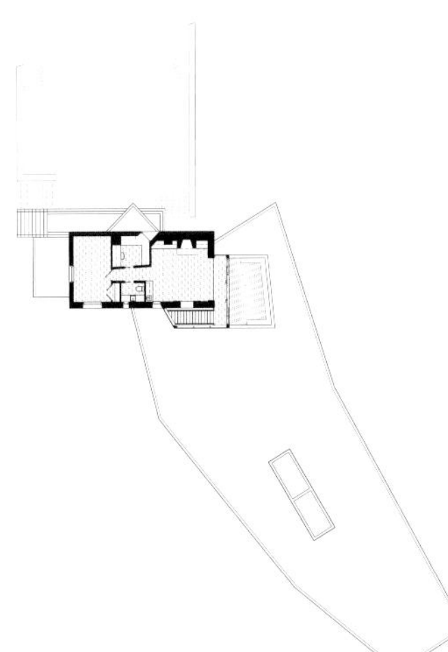

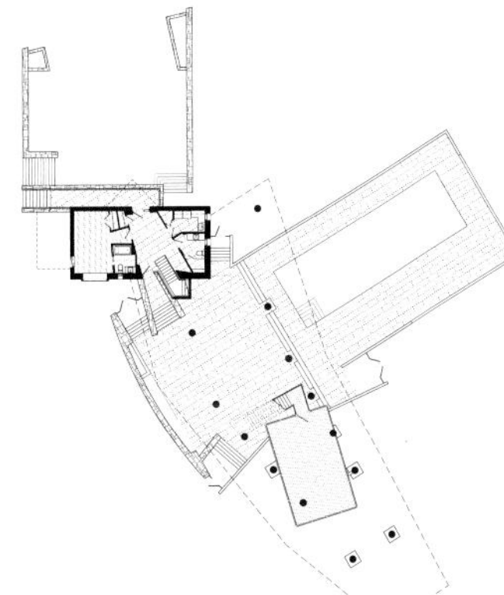

LOWER

page 216 - BAXTER/BRAY HOUSE

MAIN

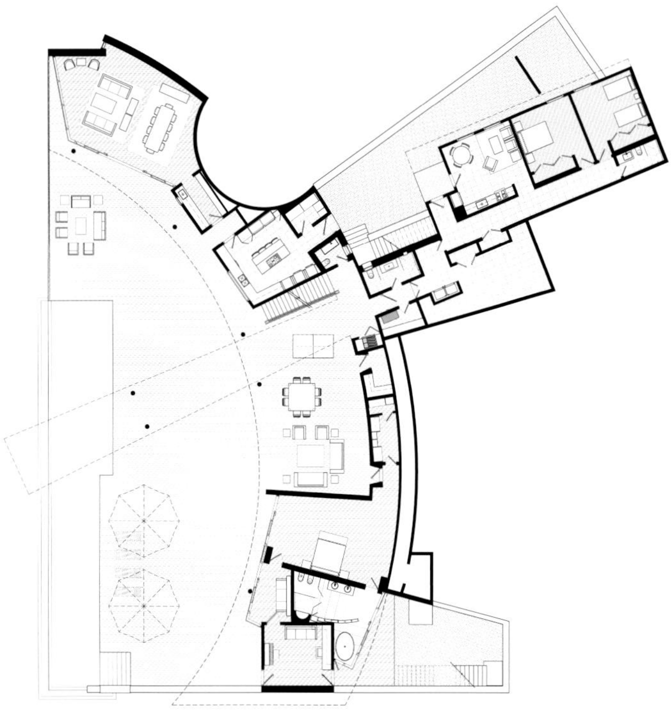

UPPER

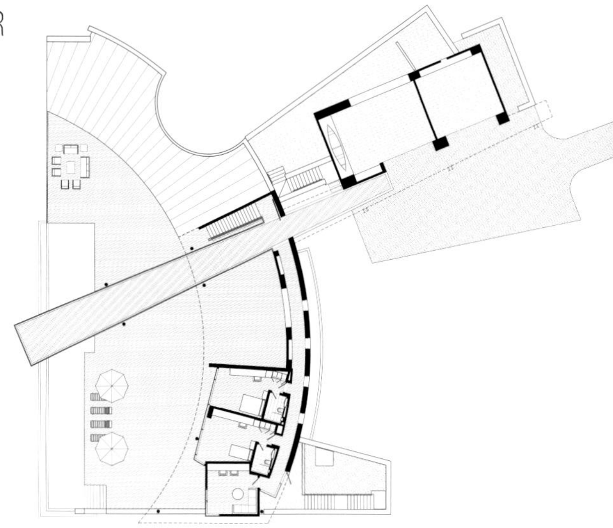

LOWER

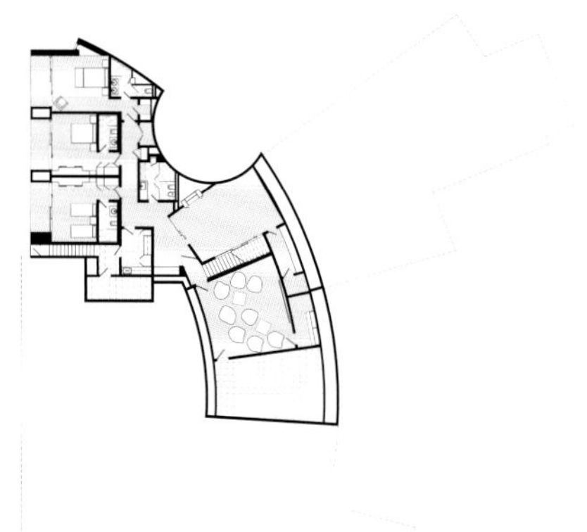

page 236 - KOCH HOUSE

MAIN

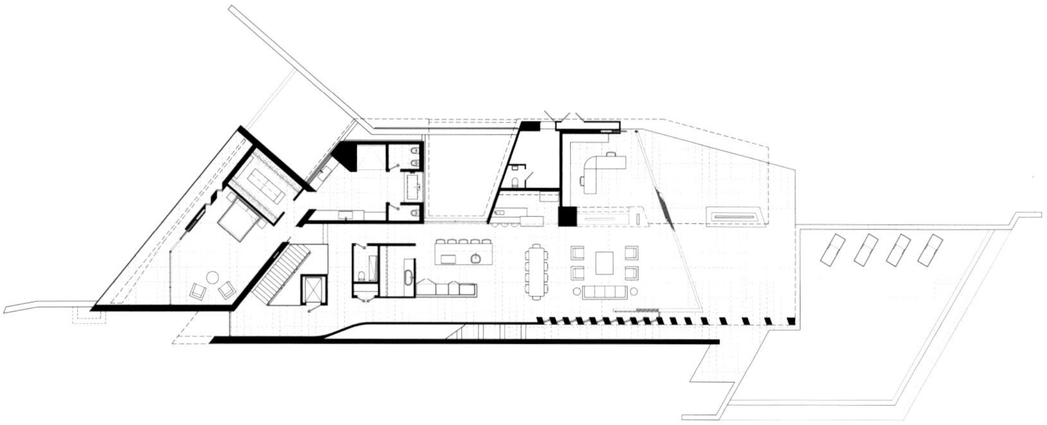

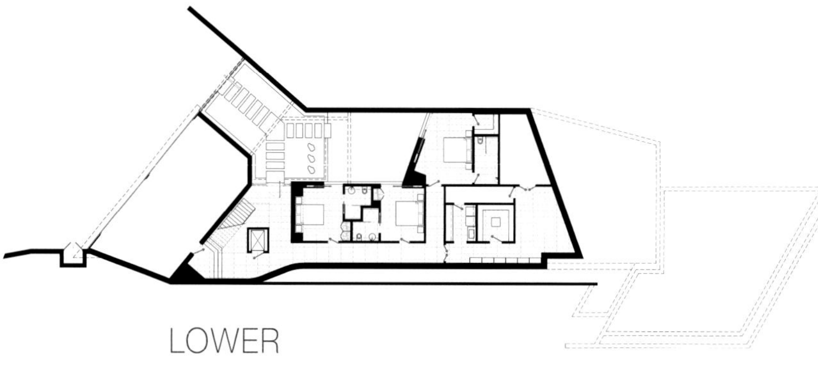

LOWER

page 258 - OWEN HOUSE

ACKNOWLEDGMENTS

As principal partner, I would like to express deep gratitude to my former partner and close friend, Robert M. Barnes, who died suddenly in 2018 and to whom this book is dedicated. Special thanks go to Alastair Gordon and Barbara de Vries of Gordon de Vries Studio, who produced this book—their erudition, wit, and dedication are evident throughout these pages—and Michael Mundy, whose beautiful photography speaks for itself. Most importantly, I wish to thank my wife, Joann Owen, for believing in me unconditionally and being my most forthright critic; my parents, James and Evelyn; and my daughter, Camille, for her love and forbearance with my work schedule while she was growing up.

—Christopher Coy

Barnes Coy Architects would like to give special thanks to our clients, without whose trust and collaborative insight we would not have been able to complete this body of work: Jay and Patty Baker, Kathryn and Garth Baxter-Bray, Arthur Beckenstein and John O'Rourke, Sheila Birnbaum and Barbara Wrubel, Justin and Melissa Boisseau, Dan and Alex Alger Chung, Jon Cohen and Karen Kostroff, George and Sharon Fontini, David Fox and Caryn Schacht, Robert and Sandy Gelfond, Robert and Lynne Grossman, Peter and Patrice Knobel, Michael and Laura Koch, Sam and Dena Lombardo, Robert Moriarty and Lisa Grattan, Elyse Nathanson, Robert Owen and Poppy LeDuc-Owen, Mitchell and Debbie Rechler, David Sack and Stephanie Segrete, Patrick and Vivian Sheil, David and Marla Susser, John and Rosanna Troiano, and Mark and Noelle Zittman.

We would like to thank our loyal staff: Esteban Mahecha, Koichi Matsumoto, Lauren Zucker, Constanza Fuentes, Chris Caruso, Charles Sferrazza, Brett Carlton, Gabrielle Robinette, Tomasz Czarnecki, Hugo Suarez, Andrew Loeshelle, Michael Spitaleri, Heidi Chi, and Emmanuel Roumeliotis.

We would also like to thank our associated designers: Michael Blake, Paul Domzal/Edgemedia, Elena Frampton, Steven Gambrel, Perry Guillot, Edmund Hollander, Tyler Horn, Mikyoung Kim, Koby Kirwin, Leonard Kowalski, Chris LaGuardia, Sue Moon, Benjamin Noriega-Ortiz, Gary Novasel, Pembrooke & Ives, Dominick Pilla, Michael Rosenberg, Julia Roth, Thomas Woltz, and Jim Wood.

Our special thanks and indebtedness go out to the late Ben Krupinski, builder extraordinaire, and the other contractors who have brought such a high level of craftsmanship to our work: Paul Consiglio, Cornerstone Construction, Thomas Johann, Cal Lavelle, Mark Lumley, Charlie Marder, Mayfair Construction, Ron Palladino, Robert Plumb, Glen Webb; Men at Work, Joseph Kelley, Jason Klinge, Cronk Duch Partners; Roderick Andersen/SARCO; John Quinn; as well as custom fabricators: Serramenti Brombal, Fleetwood, Harken, Stefan Jaeckel, Robert Kessler, Loebs & Gordon, Lynbrook Glass, Lee Miller, Cathy Smith, Tom Tebbens, Watershape, and Westhampton Architectural Glass.

Gordon de Vries Studio, the copublishers of this book, would like to give special thanks to Charles Miers, Daniel Melamud, and the editorial/production team at Rizzoli, who have been so supportive in the collaborative development of this project. We were also delighted to work in close partnership with photographer Michael Mundy who traveled far and wide to shoot every house in the book. Michael's extraordinary eye for light, form, and detail brings a warmly human sense of narrative and continuity to the architecture. We also wish to thank Shane Alzheimer, Camille Coy, Kiki Gordon, Jackie Tomlin, and everyone else who helped with the production of this publication.

First published in the United States of America in 2020 by
Rizzoli International Publications, Inc.
300 Park Avenue South
New York, NY 10010
www.rizzoliusa.com

in association with

Gordon de Vries Studio
307 Foster Hill Road
Milford, PA 18337

Design and production by Barbara de Vries
Principal photography by Michael Mundy
Additional photography by Paul Domzal/EdgeMediaDigital

For Rizzoli International Publications:
Publisher: Charles Miers
Editor: Daniel Melamud
Production: Barbara Sadick
Copy editor: Kelli Rae Patton
Proofreader: Cindy Trickel

ISBN: 978-0-8478-6858-2
Library of Congress Control Number: 2019956515

2020 2021 2022 2023 / 10 9 8 7 6 5 4 3 2 1
Printed in China

Visit us online:
Facebook.com/RizzoliNewYork
Twitter: @Rizzoli_Books
Instagram.com/RizzoliBooks
Pinterest.com/RizzoliBooks
Youtube.com/user/RizzoliNY